Alchemy in Middle-earth

**The star of Solomon's Seal
with solar and lunar symbols**

Alchemy in Middle-earth

The Significance of
J.R.R. Tolkien's
The Lord of the Rings

Mahmoud Shelton

Temple of Justice Books

Published by Temple of Justice Books
www.templeofjustice.net

Printed by Lightning Source Inc.
www.lightningsource.com

First hardcover edition 2003/1424
ISBN: 0-9741468-0-3
Library of Congress Control Number: 2003093197

Contents

As for the others, my rank is well above the dwelling place where they are established. They have no knowledge of me; they see no vestige of me. On the other hand, their dogmatic belief takes shape for them in some one of the forms of religion professed by men. They masquerade ridiculously in my name; they paint my symbol on their cheek. Then the ignorant, the inexperienced, rests his gaze there, and he imagines that indeed to be what bears the name Khidr. But how is that related to me, what have I to do with that? Or rather, what is this poor cup in relation to my jar? Unless it is said, in truth, that this is also a drop of my ocean, or an hour of my eternity, since its reality is that of a tenuous thread among my tenuities, and that the way followed by those is a way among my ways. Then, in this sense, I am also this fallacious star.[1]

~ Al-Khidr, the Green Man, known also as St. George, the patron saint of England

---

[1] Quoted in Henry Corbin, *Spiritual Body and Celestial Earth*, Princeton University Press, 1977, page 157.

Introduction

One sign of the relevance of *The Lord of the Rings* is its recent recognition as the "Novel of the Century," suggesting that this work of imagination best embodies the spirit of the present. What is more, this fantasy has persistently been compared with real events, and has become for many a touchstone in facing them. At the foundation of this phenomenon is the imagination of the author, J.R.R. Tolkien.[1] With his expertise in philology, Professor Tolkien traced the languages of his imagination to a legendary context. In developing his mythic history, Tolkien claimed that "always I had the sense of recording what was already 'there,' somewhere: not of 'inventing.'"[2] This "somewhere" is not to be reduced to the world of books with which the author was obviously familiar, since for Tolkien this place is rather a realm of truth:

> These tales are "new," they are not directly derived from other myths and legends, but they must inevitably contain a large number of ancient widespread motives or elements. After all, I believe that legends and myths are largely made of "truth," and indeed present aspects of it that can only be received in this mode; and long ago certain truths and modes of this kind were discovered and must always reappear.[3]

---

[1] All Tolkien's works cited herein are published in the United Kingdom by George Allen & Unwin and in the United States by Houghton Mufflin.

[2] *The Letters of J.R.R. Tolkien* (hereafter *Letters*), edited by Humphrey Carpenter, number 131.

[3] *Ibid.* So it may be said that the essential function of "myth" is to communicate "mysteries;" in fact the two words are related.

Although Tolkien disliked allegory, at least the deliberate allegory that is forced upon the reader, he conceded the need for allegorical language "to explain the purport of myth,"[4] and affirmed the "applicability" of his history.

The three volumes of *The Lord of the Rings* are presented as a history of Middle-earth, concerning the ending of a Third Age and the arrival of a Fourth. Middle-earth geographically approximates an ancient Europe, and even its temporal setting has some correspondence with other histories. Professor Tolkien has elaborated on his sequence of ages both in an extensive collection of appendices, and in writings for the most part published posthumously. One familiar event belonging to his Second Age is the submergence of a land to the West of Middle-earth that Tolkien calls Númenor, the Land of "Númen"[5] or the West, and since this Númenor is also and very significantly called Atalantë after its downfall, Tolkien's sequence of ages and the fall of Númenor correspond to Classical myth, for Atalantë can only be a reference to Atlantis. In fact, Tolkien always affirmed this identification, frequently calling his land "Númenor-Atlantis" in his correspondences. "Númenor is my personal alteration of the Atlantis myth and/or tradition," Tolkien once explained to his American readers, "Of all the mythical or 'archetypal' images this is the one most deeply seated in my imagination."[6] And so much of Tolkien's vision concerns the remains of his "Atlantean" tradition in Middle-earth: the works that the Men of that tradition had built dominate most of the geography of *The Lord of the Rings*, and more importantly, the last of its three volumes, *The Return of the King*, concerns the restoration of a nobility that survived the deluge.

Concerning an Atlantean "tradition," beyond the popular conception of its ancient wisdom long forgotten, there is the mythical tracing of the science of Alchemy to refugees from Atlantis.[7] Alchemy is an application of what is properly known as Hermeticism, in which

---

[4] *Ibid.*

[5] It should be observed that an association with the real word numen, signifying archetypes or ideas, is unavoidable, making Númenor in a sense a "Land of Ideas." Despite Tolkien's objections, even C.S. Lewis, his friend and fellow member of the Oxford literary circle known as the Inklings, could not ignore such an association.

[6] *Letters*, number 276.

[7] Cf. for example *Alchemy: The Art of Knowing*, Chronicle Books, 1994, page 20.

cosmological sciences operated according to a correspondence between the macrocosm of the world of appearances and the microcosm of the soul. Far from being merely a preliminary form of chemistry, Alchemy is most often occupied with the transmutation of natural materials only as the outward expression of an inward work. Because of this relationship, the scientific processes of Alchemy were naturally translated from the domain of the crafts to that of mysticism. Mysticism is not separate from religion; it is rather its inward aspect, realized in the soul. So perfection in the soul may be symbolized by gold, the perfection of metals in the language of Alchemy. Yet the cosmological sciences, when considered in themselves, address only the "lesser mysteries" and not the "greater mysteries" of mysticism, and so are really preparations for the latter. "In reality alchemy, which is not a religion by itself, required to be confirmed by the revelation – with its means of grace – which is addressed to all men;"[8] only then may the formulations of Alchemy properly be said to open onto the "greater mysteries." The word "alchemy," referring at the same time to the science of transmutation and the substance that makes it possible, is Arabic; and indeed the development of Hermeticism by Islam imprinted the science of Alchemy as an Islamic science.[9]

Hermeticism itself is traced to Hermes Trismegistos, the "Thrice-great," so called because in Islam he has been recognized in three forms. First, he is the antediluvian prophet Idris, known in the Bible as Enoch, who was raised bodily to Heaven where he maintains a high station; second, as Elias or Elijah[10], he is the prophet similarly raised on the "horse of fire;" third, he is called Hermes,[11] the teacher of the Hermetic sciences. In a more general sense, Islamic doctrine confirms the unanimity of all prophets, and the accord of their teachings: "The

[8] Titus Burckhardt, *Alchemy: Science of the Cosmos, Science of the Soul*, translated by Stoddart, Element Books, 1986, page 21.
[9] Cf. Seyyed Hossein Nasr, *Islamic Science: An Illustrated Study*, World of Islam Festival, 1976, chapter IX. The word "alchemy" is further related to a Chinese etymology, although more commonly the word is traced to "Khem," the "Black Land" of Egypt.
[10] Cf. the chapter concerning Elias in the *Fusus al-Hikam* of Ibn al-`Arabi.
[11] Cf. Humphrey Carpenter's *J.R.R. Tolkien: A Biography* for a curious mention of Hermes in Tolkien's early life (page 57). Mercury is but the Roman name for Hermes; according to Julius Caesar, Mercury was foremost in the religious perspective of the ancient inhabitants of Britain.

messenger believeth in that which hath been revealed unto him from his Lord, and so do the faithful. Each one believeth in God and His angels and His books and His messengers – there is no sundering the unity of the messengers."[12] So the sciences of Hermes were renewed in the light of the new revelation of Islam, a revelation that moreover confirms Muhammad to be the last and the Seal of the Prophets.

J.R.R. Tolkien was himself a practicing Catholic, whose professional concerns at Oxford University were the languages and heroic literature of Northern Europe in the Middle Ages. Although Tolkien's "history" pretends to concern an ancient Earth, its anachronisms are many, and its setting recalls rather that of Medieval Europe on the eve of another age, a Renaissance. It was during this historical period that Alchemy passed in its Islamic formulation to the Jewish and Christian communities. Alchemy's language is purely symbolic, and because of its treatment of cosmology not theology, its language was easily shared. Such a language should be invaluable for Tolkien the philologist, for whom the reconciliation of his Classical and other pre-Christian sources with his own faith was a real concern. Many of Shakespeare's works contain an alchemical language in relating "histories" of the Middle Ages, and while Tolkien was critical of Shakespeare, this was because he felt, apparently, that he should have done better; indeed some motifs in *The Lord of the Rings* are obviously offered as improvements on Shakespeare's art. What is remarkable is how unrecognized the alchemical language is in Tolkien's great work, even though some of the greatest names in the heritage of Alchemy in Christian Europe are very closely associated with Oxford, and will be mentioned in due course.

For indeed *The Lord of the Rings* is an essentially "alchemical" work, with its imagery of fire and metallurgy, and more importantly, "transmutation" from one state of existence to another. More exactly, the author presents in its events the symbolism of an alchemical process. The story literally traces a quest to unmake a great evil embodied in a magic ring. The fact that the quest is to unmake rather than obtain such an object seems to be a mythic innovation, yet it is perfectly in accordance with the science of Alchemy, which always demands the unmaking of a material before transmutation is possible. Moreover, *The Lord of the Rings* shares its fantastic imagery with the stories of Hermetic inspiration,

---

[12] *Qur'an* II, 285.

which were often fantastic and abstruse; such conventions exemplify Tolkien's "truths and modes." Alchemical literature even developed ciphers to veil its secrets. No doubt the symbolic language of Alchemy always demanded rather an inward vision to decode its true meanings. So at least Tolkien's particular obsession in creating languages for his fantasy should not be trivialized; indeed the exactness with which he arrived at names and the meanings at their roots "grew from his belief in the ultimate *truth* of his mythology."[13]

It is not simply owing to the Islamic heritage of Alchemy that the teachings of Islam should be considered in the study of *The Lord of the Rings*. Since the story relates the "history" of an end of an age, it should therefore not be at all surprising that it resonates with eschatology; Tolkien admitted that history "contains (and in a legend may contain more clearly and movingly) some samples or glimpses of final victory,"[14] that is, of eschatology. Now the eschatology of Islam is especially rich, due to Islam's heralded position as the last revelation; it is in light of this eschatology that *The Lord of the Rings* reveals a rather unexpected applicability. It is through the eyes of the Hobbits, a "little people" invented by Tolkien, that the reader is witness to the story's eschatological events. The Hobbits' simple virtues mirror the virtues of rural England, when in Tolkien's day traditional English life was under threat by the chaotic forces of modernization. Indeed Tolkien's vision is profoundly traditional, and it is precisely the authenticity of traditional virtues that he champions against the darkness of the end of an age. The present work is concerned more with what Tolkien calls "the story and its symbolism"[15] than with moral virtues that are universal and require no commentary. For in the study of the significance of the former aspects Tolkien's real "alchemy" becomes apparent, shining through the veil of fantasy that forms only the appearance of *The Lord of the Rings*.

---

[13] Carpenter, *op. cit.*, page 102.
[14] *Letters*, number 195.
[15] *Ibid.*, number 142.

4	9	2
3	5	7
8	1	6

Talismanic Square

1

Ring of Darkness

In the imaginary history of the Third Age of Middle-earth in *The Lord of the Rings*, the marshalling of the world into two armies, of good and of evil, becomes ever more clear. This opposition is personified in two principal characters: the Dark Lord Sauron, who seeks the One Ruling Ring, and Gandalf the Wizard. Now the significance of the latter's epithets requires some explanation, and here the originality of Tolkien's vision must be acknowledged. First, for the philologist, "wizard" simply means "wise," in contradistinction to "sorcerer," a title by which Sauron is identified; certainly for Tolkien, a wizard is something much more than a conjurer. Second, according to the author's etymology, Gandalf means "Staff-Elf." Here as always the image of Tolkien's Elves is separated from fairy tales, becoming instead an image of a humanity of glorious excellence, luminous and immortal and free from the fears and afflictions of fallen men. Such a description accords remarkably well with that of religious sainthood; for example, saints are described in the Holy Qur'an as those "upon whom there is neither fear nor affliction."[1] It is said of the Elves: "'They do not fear the Ringwraiths, for those who have lived in the Blessed Realm live at once in both worlds, and against both the Seen and the Unseen they have great power.'"[2] Again in the Holy Qur'an, God is named the "Knower of the Seen and Unseen," and so in Islam there are essentially two forms of knowledge, that of the Visible and that of the Hidden,[3] or of bodies and of spirits. This

---

[1] X, 62.

[2] "Many Meetings," *The Fellowship of the Ring*.

[3] The proper relationship of the Seen and Unseen is called in Islamic Alchemy the "balance," a doctrine emphasized especially by Jabir Ibn Hayyan, whose corpus "is the most important single body of works on alchemy in Arabic and the main

distinction may be compared with the Classical formulation of the lesser and greater mysteries. In Islamic mysticism or Sufism, command of both forms of knowledge is an attribute of the saint, who is sometimes called the "Lord of the Two Eyes." The saints are those about whom it is said, "Our spirits have become materialized and our material bodies spiritualized,"[4] and who therefore live "at once in both worlds." So "Elf" becomes more than a reference to race, since "Staff-Elf" the Wizard is not an Elf; he came to Middle-earth from the "Blessed Realm," however, and his staff signifies his rank.[5]

In *The Fellowship of the Ring*, Gandalf faces a demon of fire called a Balrog in the Mines of Moria, and in opposing this demon passes through a death and resurrection as Gandalf the White. Here is a depiction of the stages of the alchemical work known respectively as that of "blackening" or death, followed by that of "whitening." Yet with his appearance as the White, Gandalf is specifically called "Mithrandir," a name in which the name of Mithra is likewise unmistakable. Now the solar cult of Mithra, arising from ancient Persia, enacted a death and resurrection in its initiatory rituals, which were moreover carried out in grottos. A strange iconographic figure belonging to Mithraism is that of its Aeon, a winged, lion-headed man with a sword, whose legs are bound by a serpent. All of these elements are present in Gandalf's confrontation with the Balrog in the cavern of Moria: the demon is winged, with a mane and sword, whose whip recalls the serpent in its binding of Gandalf's knees. The descent with the Balrog "into the deep water" and "to the uttermost foundations of stone," followed by the spiraling ascent of the "Endless Stair" to a "dizzy eyrie above the mists of the world" where the Balrog "burst into new flame," may be

---

source not only of Islamic alchemy but even to a large extent of Latin alchemy" (Nasr, *op. cit.*, page 199).

[4] In this context, that the Elves leave "no footprint" is evidence of their "spiritualized bodies." The Prophet of Islam is remembered as leaving no footprint in the sand.

[5] It must be admitted that Tolkien often called Gandalf "angelic," both because the meaning of the term describes the role of a "messenger" – likewise its significance in the Semitic languages – and because there are for Tolkien "no precise modern terms to say what he was" (*Letters*, number 156), and this is unfortunately the case for modern Catholicism, with its reformed sense of sainthood. It should moreover be noted that the role of divine messenger corresponds to that of Hermes-Mercury in Classical mythology.

compared with the following description of the Aeon: "He who made all things and governs all things, joined together by means of the surrounding Heaven the power and nature of Water and Earth, heavy and downward, flowing down into the Depth, and that of Fire and Spirit, light and rushing up to the measureless Height."[6] The "resurrected" Mithrandir unveils himself upon a rock, whereas Mithra was said to have been born from a rock; indeed, in his resurrected form, he answers only to Mithrandir, while affirming "'I was Gandalf.'" Tolkien's descriptions evoke very precisely Mithraic ritual; yet these motifs should not be considered independent from alchemical symbolism, when Alchemy historically preserved Mithraic formulations in its treatment of "death" and "resurrection."

Since the name of Tolkien's demon is constructed of the two elements "Bal" and "rog," and because of the solar emphasis of Mithraism, it may be observed that the first element recalls the name of the pagan sun-god Baal of the ancient Near East, and so Mithrandir and the Balrog suggest two aspects of solar symbolism. Their precise opposition is in fact confirmed by their equivalence on Tolkien's imaginary chain of being, for although respectively "angelic" and "demonic," Mithrandir and the Balrog are both "Maiar." This coincidence with the pagan sun-god is mentioned not least because it was particularly the prophet Elias – one of the forms of the Thrice-Great Hermes - who opposed the worship of Baal in his time. In the ascension of Elias on the "horse of fire" according to the history of at-Tabari, "God covered him in feathers, clothed him in fire, and stopped for him the pleasure of food and drink. He flew with the angels, becoming human-angelic, earthly-heavenly."[7] Indeed in his resurrected form, Gandalf flies with the Lord of the Eagles, who describes his new "human-angelic, earthly-heavenly" identity: "'Light as a swan's feather in my claw you are. The Sun shines through you…were I to let you fall, you would float upon the wind.'"[8] Since in Hermeticism the Aeon takes the form of a bird, the resurrection of Mithrandir also establishes that there are two

[6] "The White Rider," *The Two Towers*; and Macrobius, quoted in G.R.S. Mead, *Thrice-Greatest Hermes. Studies in Hellenistic Theosophy and Gnosis.*

[7] *The History of al-Tabari, Volume III: The Children of Israel*, translated by Brinner, SUNY, 1991, page 125.

[8] "The White Rider."

aspects to the Aeon or Time, maleficent like the Balrog and beneficent like the Lord of Eagles.

In his confrontation with the Balrog, Gandalf declares, "I am a servant of the Secret Fire, wielder of the flame of Anor. You cannot pass. The dark fire will not avail you, flame of Udûn..."[9] The association of fire with ancient Persia recalls the Magi, for whom fire was the most sacred element; yet it should be recognized that fire dominates the perspective of all metallurgical crafts, including Alchemy. Here two opposing fires and flames are distinguished, respectively "dark" and "secret" or inward. This distinction is sufficiently explained in the teachings of Najmuddin Kubra, who said, "Our way is the way of Alchemy;" a master of Persian Sufism, Kubra addressed the subject of dhikr or "remembrance of God" according to Sufism's inward understanding: "As opposed to the fire of the Devil, which is a dark fire...the fire of the dhikr is visualized as a pure and ardent blaze...This fire enters into the dwelling place like a sovereign prince, announcing: 'I alone, and none other than I.' It sets fire to all that there is to be consumed, and sheds light on any darkness it may encounter."[10] It must also be remembered that the term "Secret Fire" specifically belongs to the alchemical writings of Paracelsus. This fire is even called by alchemists their "sun," which is the significance of Tolkien's word Anor. And the term "Anor" is especially significant here, since Tolkien establishes its root to be "nar," his Elvish word for fire; yet "nar" is in reality the Arabic word for fire.

The One Ruling Ring of the Dark Lord Sauron and the staff of Gandalf, the "Enemy of Sauron," find their proper archetypes in one of the "signs" of Islamic eschatology. Commenting on the Beast of the Earth mentioned in the Holy Qur'an[11], Traditions relate that the Beast will carry the Ring of Solomon and the Staff of Moses, and with the Ring will mark the unbeliever with darkness, and with the Staff will mark the believer with a white spot which will expand until the face of the believer is shining like a star. The association of Gandalf's staff with the Staff of Moses is by no means accidental. Just as Islamic sources attribute the power of casting light in the darkness to Moses' Staff, so does

---

[9] "The Bridge of Khazad-Dûm," *The Fellowship of the Ring*.
[10] Quoted in Henry Corbin, *The Man of Light in Iranian Sufism*, Shambhala, 1978, page 74.
[11] XXVII, 85

Gandalf's staff light the path through Moria. What is more, in the confrontation at court of Gandalf with the "snake" Wormtongue – and Wormtongue's particular fear of the staff – recalls Moses' vanquishing of the snakes of the sorcerers of the Pharaoh with his Staff. It is significant that the Staff is one of Nine Signs given to Moses. Another is the "White Hand"[12] that appears in *The Lord of the Rings* as the insignia of Saruman the White, the head of the Order of Wizards before Gandalf becomes the White.[13] For Saruman abandons the white of purity for the disunity of many colors, and his continued use of the White Hand insignia is in caricature of his original function. Saruman's role as the master of Wormtongue identifies him with the Pharaoh; for indeed he is very like the Pharaoh who is seen in Islam as having abandoned his saintly identity for that of a tyrant.

The nature of evil in *The Lord of the Rings* is peculiarly as the counterfeit and perversion of good. It is, of course, appropriate to associate the One Ring of Sauron with the Ring of Solomon. Religious histories identify this Ring as being from Paradise, and that it is the source of Solomon's absolute authority on Earth; yet it becomes lost for a time to a devil who causes corruption in Solomon's place. It is eventually returned to its rightful owner from a watery resting place by means of a fish. In Tolkien's history of events leading to *The Lord of the Rings*, twice the ring of Sauron is recovered from watery circumstances when fishing or a fish is recalled at the same time: first when Gollum finds the ring, and later in *The Hobbit* when Bilbo comes to possess it. Yet unlike that of Solomon, Tolkien's ring is not lost to a devil, but rather lost by one. Without doubt, the infernal ring of Sauron's making must be seen clearly as the parody of the Paradise Ring of Solomon, since it unifies the world in corruption – "and in the darkness bind them" - and so mocks the unity of Solomon's absolute authority. The ring of the Dark Lord is a ring

---

[12] *Qur'an* VII, 108. The talismanic significance of the hand is universally recognized.

[13] The conflict of Mithrandir and the fallen Saruman evokes the opposition of Mithra and the Luciferian Ahriman in Persian legend. However, in an Ottoman mystical epic, the Saltuqname, Ahriman takes the form of a lion-headed devil, and so is related to the Balrog.

of darkness, and its golden appearance betokens only darkness in the world, not the luminous gold of Alchemy.[14]

The winged mounts of the Ringwraiths – Sauron's most terrible servants - are a twisted mockery of the supernatural Eagles that bring assistance from above. The Orc soldiers of the "Enemy" are identified as genetically engineered counterfeits of the Elves, the luminous "People of the Stars." Gandalf the White opposes the Dark Lord; the White Tower of Gondor opposes the Dark Tower of Sauron; and the White Council of Wizards and Elves was convened to oppose the Dark Lord and his designs. This Council of the Wise strongly suggests the Diwan al-awliya', or Council of the Saints, in Islamic mysticism. Indeed, all this embodies the distinction between the saints – the Friends of God - and their counterfeit, the "Friends of Satan." According to the Holy Qur'an: "Allah is the protecting Friend of those who believe. He bringeth them out of darkness into light. As for those who disbelieve, their patrons are the false. They bring them out of light into darkness."[15]

The widely known "magic square" of the first nine numbers has been traced to the "Temple of Light" of ancient China. In Alchemy it is a talisman of the greatest importance, as it conveys the numerology of the "balance" according to Jabir Ibn Hayyan.[16] This arrangement has even been seen to contain the numerology of the ranks of the saints in Sufism.[17] It is therefore not without significance that this talisman has a relationship with the epigraph of *The Lord of the Rings*:

> Three Rings for the Elven-kings under the sky,
> > Seven for the Dwarf-lords in their halls of stone,
> Nine for Mortal Men doomed to die,
> > One for the Dark Lord on his dark throne...

---

[14] Following the example of the Prophet Muhammad, men in Islam refuse to wear golden rings.

[15] II, 257.

[16] This talisman establishes that seventeen is the "key to the understanding of the structure of the world" (Nasr, *op. cit.*, page 195). This number is unmistakably in the structure of *The Lord of the Rings*. To provide but one example, seventeen is the number of years that pass between the first and second chapters.

[17] Cf. Sir Jehangir C. Coyagee's *Cults and Legends of Ancient Iran and China*, pages 166-7.

Here the numbers of the Rings of Power belonging to Elves, Men, and Dwarves, as well as the Dark Lord, are arranged at every side of the central and therefore superior position that is occupied by the number five.[18] Significantly, the Order of Wizards sent to oppose Sauron in Middle-earth, and arrange those with the will to resist him, was composed of five members. Five is likewise the number of Poles (Aqtab) at the head of the hierarchy of saints in Islam.[19] Since the talismanic hand itself signifies five, it may be said that the foremost of the five Wizards whose insignia is the White Hand is himself represented by the 5 in this talisman. For this reason, the corruption of Saruman appears especially pernicious, and Gandalf's attainment of that central position very important indeed.

While nine may apply to the ranks of saints, its inverse application is recalled in the following verse: "And there were in the city nine who did corruption in the land and reformed not."[20] Of course, this number is well represented in *The Lord of the Rings* by the Nine Ringwraiths who were themselves formerly lords among Men. This perversion of human nobility in the service of evil is in turn precisely

---

[18] It is also interesting to observe that the corner positions are excluded from this formula, because in the system of substituting letters for numbers, these four corner positions spell out the name of this magic square in Arabic. In fact, this name is a talisman by itself.

[19] While the five Wizards may recall the five Aqtab, the figure of Tom Bombadil approximates that class of saints called the Afrad, or "Solitaries," who are alone among saints in having authority seemingly independent of the Aqtab. Regarding the curious description of Bombadil as "oldest and fatherless," it should be mentioned that according to Islamic mysticism, there has been not one Adam – likewise "oldest and fatherless" – but no less than 100,000 Adams in cyclic succession on Earth. It should also be observed that the black magic from which Bombadil frees the Hobbits in "Fog on the Barrow-downs" (*The Fellowship of the Ring*) is a vivid depiction of a "dark Alchemy" opposite to the true science. In this false Alchemy, the Hobbits are imprisoned in a tomb, clothed in white and ornamented with gold, with their souls being cursed instead of healed. Significantly, the breaking of this spell demands the offering of the golden hoard in charity, after which Bombadil gives the Hobbits a vision of that lineage through which true Alchemy will be accomplished for Middle-earth: "...a vision as it were of a vast expanse of years behind them, like a vast shadowy plain over which there strode shapes of Men, tall and grim with bright swords, and last came one with a star on his brow."

[20] *Qur'an* XXVII, 48.

opposed by the Fellowship of Nine sent by the Wise to undo the work of the Enemy. Twenty-seven as an extension of nine has a further importance, since in the teachings of Islam, twenty-seven are the types of prophetic inheritances or wisdoms belonging to the saints. This relationship is formulated in the Tradition of the Prophet of Islam: "The wise are the heirs of the prophets." The explanation of this relationship was brought to perfection in the twenty-seven chapters of the *Fusus al-Hikam* ("Bezels of Wisdom") of the Great Master of Islamic mysticism, Muhyiuddin Ibn al-`Arabi[21]; and in this great work, ring stones symbolize these inheritances. Significantly, the rings of the Wise in *The Lord of the Rings* each have a unique stone, whereas the ring of the Dark Lord has none. In this connection, and on the other hand, another Tradition holds that twenty-seven "Imposters" among the Friends of Satan precede the rise of the final Imposter, the Antichrist.[22] The appearance of this Imposter – the Dajjal - is indeed another of the eschatological signs in Islam. It is therefore very remarkable indeed that the Dark Lord of Tolkien's imagination only appears as the Eye, that is moreover his insignia and mark, for the most distinguishing mark of the Dajjal in the Traditions of Islam is that he likewise has but one eye.

---

[21] "Ibn `Arabi...had a profound influence on medieval alchemists" (*Alchemy: The Art of Knowing*, page 20).
[22] Michel Chodkiewicz, *Seal of the Saints: Prophethood and Sainthood in the Doctrine of Ibn 'Arabi*, Islamic Texts Society, 1993, pages 86-7.

2

Sword and Stone

In Islamic sources the Staff of Moses is identified as being forked. The Prophet of Islam is called "Owner of the Staff," and this name is of interest since it is regarded among those foretelling his appearance in the Christian Gospel. Here the staff is not that of Moses; it is properly a "staff of iron," or rather a sword.[1] What is more, the name particularly refers to the "Rider on a White Horse" from the eschatological Book of Revelation, an image that relates to *The Lord of the Rings*, since Gandalf is the "White Rider" who wields both staff and sword. The most renowned sword of the Prophet has always been depicted as having a forked point; this sword Dhul-Fiqar was later the sign of `Ali, the first Imam of the Family of the Prophet Muhammad, and so it is a tradition in Islamic mysticism: "There is no chivalrous youth if not `Ali, there is no sword if not Dhul-Fiqar."[2] The form of this sword has thus been perpetuated in many surviving Islamic sword blades. Like the emblem of Hermes or Mercury called the caduceus, with its two serpents balanced around a staff, all these instruments of authority represent the regulation of a fundamental duality by a transcendent unity, with the influence of this unity belonging to the axial or polar dimension.

---

[1] Cf. Qadi `Iyad, *Ash-Shifa* (translated as *Muhammad Messenger of Allah* by Bewley, Madinah Press, 1991), "On his names and their excellence."

[2] "It is said that Sayidna `Ali had a perfect knowledge of alchemy in all its aspects, including those related to the production of outward effects, such as metallic transmutations, but that he always refused to make use of them" (René Guénon, *Perspectives on Initiation*, Sophia Perennis, 2001, page 262 note 16).

Alchemy calls the terms of the cosmic duality sulphur and quicksilver, and depicts them as sun and moon.[3] This duality, the terms of which are strictly speaking complementary, is expressed in so many symbolic pairings, all of which correspond on some level to the more fundamental terms of Heaven and Earth. The union of Heaven and Earth belongs above all to the example of the holy prophets who offered Heavenly guidance on Earth, such as Idris and Moses and Muhammad. This is likewise the example of Dhul-Qarnain, the "Lord of the Two Horns," mentioned in the Holy Qur'an and identified in Islam with Alexander the Great. The Prophet of Islam is called the Lord of the Two Realms. A sword of the Prophet preserved in the Ottoman Palace of Topkapi,[4] while without a forked point, nevertheless has serpentine quillons on either side of its handle, so again recalling the caduceus and the transcending of duality.

In the Second Age of Middle-earth that precedes the events of *The Lord of the Rings*,[5] the Last Alliance of Elves and Men faced the Dark Lord on the battlefield. Elendil, the King of the Númenórean refugees in Middle-earth, was the ruler of two realms: Arnor in the North and Gondor in the South. This "Elf-friend" wielded the sword Narsil, a name that signifies the light of both the sun and moon. The names of Elendil's two sons, Anárion and Isildur, hold the same significance. So Elendil, whose name signifies "Star-lover," unites the complementary symbols of sun and moon that are embodied in the name Narsil and so also in the names Anárion and Isildur.[6] Indeed in alchemical symbolism, the star is positioned between the opposing sun and moon. This relationship is geographically expressed in Gondor with its three original cities: Minas

---

[3] In the designation "Temple of Light" for the talismanic square discussed above, the Chinese character for "light" is composed of two elements that signify respectively "sun" and "moon."

[4] Having been preserved in the Caliphal Treasury, this sword is possibly to be identified with one mentioned in the histories as originating in the "time of `Ad;" this expression has been identified by Donnelly as an Arabian expression for Atlantean culture (*Atlantis: The Antediluvian World*, Gramercy, 1949).

[5] The relevant accounts of the ages prior to the Third Age are contained both in appendix A of *The Lord of the Rings* and in the posthumously published *The Silmarillion*.

[6] In appendix A, Tolkien also mentions a "great white pillar" established as a memorial of victory against Sauron "that took the rays of the Sun and of the Moon and shone like a bright star."

Anor, the "Tower of the Western Sun;" Minas Ithil, the "Tower of the Rising Moon;" and between them on the river Anduin, Osgiliath, "Citadel of the Stars," the chief city of Gondor.

On the battlefield, when Elendil was slain by Sauron, his sword was broken and its light was extinguished. Yet with this broken sword Isildur cut the One Ring from Sauron's hand, and possession of the ring thus becomes a sinister compensation for the loss of Elendil. The moon, that either reflects light or becomes dark, is used in traditional cosmology as a symbol of the world with its changing fortunes. In the loss of the light of Elendil, that which relates to Isildur is particularly affected, since Isildur is associated with the moon and so to the "passivity" of the lunar aspect. So the One Ring acquired through the loss of Elendil becomes "Isildur's Bane,"[7] and Minas Ithil, cut off from the Tower of the Sun, is conquered by the Dark Lord to become the Ringwraiths' Tower of Sorcery. Furthermore, the alchemical work must begin with the preparation of the "lunar" material, before the "solar" aspect may be restored. So it is the line of Isildur that retreats into obscurity with the Sword that was Broken, until the reforging of the sword by the heir of Isildur.

The reforging of the sword Narsil reunites the lights of the sun and the moon, and indeed the conjunction of the sun and moon is a goal of the alchemical work. This particular conjunction is in fact accomplished by Elven smiths; the sword is thereafter borne by the heir of Isildur as an emblem of an inheritance yet to be fully realized.[8] Nevertheless, the sword of Elendil is reforged in the first volume of *The Lord of the Rings*, before Middle-earth may be healed of Sauron's corruption; for this reason the reforging of the sword announces a transcendent authorization for war. The Sword Reforged is renamed

---

[7] Still, it should not be overlooked that Isildur himself seems essentially incorruptible, since the ring so quickly abandons him, unlike any other of its bearers.

[8] The correspondence between Elendil and his heir is made more and more clear as the story unfolds. For example, when the Fellowship of the Ring passes in their quest on the river Anduin between the Pillars of the Kings, representations of Anárion and Isildur, only the bearer of Elendil's sword passes without fear, so recalling the Qur'anic description of sainthood, and "a light was in his eyes," just as the legacy of Elendil was manifested in his two luminous sons. Concerning the two realms of Elendil, his heir affirms, "'I belong both to Gondor and the North'" ("Flotsam and Jetsam," *The Two Towers*).

Andúril, signifying "flame," and so Andúril is a flaming sword; Dhul-Fiqar likewise appears as a flaming sword in Islamic heroic legend. At the same time Andúril reunites the names of *Anárion*, *Isildur*, and *Elendil*. Inscribed on its blade are the symbols of sun and crescent moon, and appropriately positioned between them, stars. In the language of Alchemy, it is preeminently the star of six points formed by the intersection of two triangles that depicts the union of the heavenly and the earthly.[9] This talisman, known as the Seal of Solomon, often appears in Ottoman military iconography; in fact the Ottoman ruler was extolled with all these emblems: "The unique universal ruler, the sun illuminating the entire heaven, the moon-like king of the nine-fold arches, the illustrious lord, ornament of the Solomonic throne...who bears Solomon's starry emblem."[10] The Seal of Solomon is a recurrent motif on Islamic sword blades, a convention still preserved in the ceremonial swords of the American Army and Marines. In a remarkable flag from a Polish collection,[11] this talisman (frontispiece) surmounts the image of the two-pointed sword of the Prophet, while another six-pointed star decorates the sword's hilt; of course, it is from the hilt that the sword is wielded and the two points of the blade, as well as its two serpentine quillons, are united. These symbols are moreover surrounded by depictions of crescent moons united with suns.[12]

Specifically, there are seven stars inscribed on the blade of Andúril.[13] The motif of seven stars refers to Tolkien's Second Age, when Elendil and his captains escaped the downfall of Númenor.

Tall ships and tall kings

---

[9] Although this symbol appears on Islamic amulets in the ninth century C.E., "in the Jewish religion it did not become widespread before the sixteenth century," that is, well after the spread of Islamic Alchemy (Zdzisław Żygulski, Jr., *Islamic Art in the Service of Empire*, New York University, 1992, page 43).
[10] Quoted in Emel Esın, "Turkic and Ilkhanid Universal Monarch Representations and the Cakravartin," *Proceedings of the Twenty-sixth International Congress of Orientalists*, 1968, page 120.
[11] Reproduced in Żygulski, page 47.
[12] Since the sun and moon may be replaced by the combat of the dragon and phoenix, this alternative motif also appears in alchemical symbolism.
[13] The constellation of seven stars is a common motif on Chinese sword blades. It should also be mentioned that the sword and seven stars are symbols appearing in the Book of Revelation.

> Three times three,
> What brought they from the foundered land
> Over the flowing sea?
> Seven stars and seven stones
> And one white tree.[14]

"Three times three" is a fundamental alchemical expression that relates to the talismanic square already considered, and so returns to the significance of nine, that here is the number of sailing vessels. Seven of these ships sailed under the sign of the star, marking that each carried one of the seven Seeing-stones, or palantíri. These crystal balls were gifts of the Elves to the refugees from Númenor, through which communication could be maintained between the Númenórean rulers throughout Middle-earth.

Now the deluge of Atlantis corresponds in Abrahamic faith to the flood that the prophet Noah survived in his Ark.[15] For this reason, the following Tradition becomes especially significant when considering Elendil – whom Tolkien calls "Noachian"[16] - and his captains: "The world after Noah has never been without seven people through which God wards off evil from humankind."[17] Indeed, the star has two symbolic aspects in Islam, to guide[18] or to ward off evil as a "shooting star." It is in the latter aspect that the star becomes a "stone," which explains "seven stars" for "seven stones." The forging of meteoric iron may be understood as an assimilation of this aspect, and this may be

---

[14] "The Palantír," *The Two Towers*.

[15] At the same time, Plato's source for his account of Atlantis and the earliest traces of Alchemy are Egyptian, and Tolkien no doubt is making reference to Egypt with the name of the last ruler of Númenor, Ar-Pharazôn, whose doom corresponds closely with the example of the Pharaoh in the Old Testament and the Holy Qur'an. Tolkien specifically compared the Númenórean penchant for monumental building with that of ancient Egypt (*Letters*, number 211), and it is significant that Egyptian sources trace the building of its temples to seven enlightened survivors of a flooded island (Graham Hancock and Robert Bauval, *The Message of the Sphinx*, Three Rivers, 1996, pages 200-1). The building of the pyramids is attributed in Islamic sources to the antediluvian form of Hermes.

[16] *Letters*, number 131.

[17] Quoted in *Islamic Doctrines & Beliefs, Volume 1*, As-Sunna Foundation of America, 1999, page 125.

[18] The Prophet Muhammad is reported to have said, "My companions are like stars; whomsoever you follow, you will be rightly guided."

extended to the depiction of seven stars on the sword Andúril. The constellation of seven stars has from very ancient times signified the presence of saints. René Guénon, the great scholar of the science of symbolism, has focused on the relationships between seven-star constellations and the seven "lights" who preserve wisdoms from age to age.[19]

The Ship of the Seven

In Christianity and Islam alike, such a seven-fold sainthood is found in the history of the Companions of the Cave. The miraculous preservation of these seven youths against the unbelief of a passing age relates clearly to the significance of the seven stars for Guénon. Yet it is especially in Islam that an even more remarkable relationship exists between the symbolism of Elendil and the formulation of the

---

[19] Cf. especially "The Wild Boar and the Bear" in *Fundamental Symbols of Sacred Science*, in which Guénon mentions a transference from the polar significance of the Great Bear to the Atlantean significance of the Pleiades.

Companions of the Cave. In Islamic mysticism, a popular form of talisman is composed of the names of these seven saints; and these names are traditionally written out in the form of a ship, explicitly recalling the Noachian aspect of preserving sanctity in a time of unbelief. A less historical aspect of this seven-fold sainthood in Islam concerns the cosmological division of the Earth into seven regions, a division that reflects the structure of the seven Heavens. In this traditional cosmology, each division is assigned to the authority of one of seven saints, who in turn represents one of the seven prophets in the Heavenly order. Each of these saints is in communication with the others, and all are under the authority of the leader of the seven, who represents the prophet Idris. The positioning of the palantíri throughout the realm of Elendil and his sons is a tangible expression of this belief in the spiritual government of the world that guides and protects.[20]

However, the practice of scrying with crystal balls belongs explicitly to the Alchemy of the Renaissance. Doctor John Dee in particular claimed to gain knowledges preserved from the antediluvian world in this fashion, and one of his scrying instruments was even brought from the New World that he identified with Atlantis. Tolkien's Seeing-stones, of course, are brought over the sea from Númenor-Atlantis. What is more, the matter of Seeing-stones may be uncovered from the heritage of Tolkien's own Oxford University. Elias Ashmole,[21] whose name has great distinction at Oxford University to this day, took great interest in the scrying of Dr. Dee. Ashmole described a variety of stones belonging to the science of Alchemy, including a Seeing-stone that enabled its owner to investigate the affairs of the Earth. Remarkably, concerning the "Angelic Stone," he maintained that only Hermes, Moses, and Solomon understood its use, and so the association of the Seeing-

---

[20] In "The Window on the West" (*The Two Towers*), Tolkien associates the character of the Númenóreans with that of Wizards, suggesting a relationship with the saints known as the Aqtab or Poles mentioned earlier in connection with the Order of Wizards.

[21] Ashmole served the Stuart monarch of Great Britain as official historian of the Order of the Garter. It is of interest, then, to acknowledge Tolkien's work in translating "Sir Gawain and the Green Knight," which offers an unofficial account of the Order's origin. Cf. the introduction to *The Royal Book of Spiritual Chivalry* (Kazi, 2000) on the significance of this account from an Islamic perspective. In addition, the development of Rosicrucian Hermeticism seems to have been linked to the Order of the Garter.

stones of Alchemy with the prophets of Islam already belongs to the heritage of Oxford. Tolkien revives this heritage by making his palantíri the instruments by which saintly communion is established.

D.ᴿ DEE avoucheth his Seras is brought by Angelical Ministry.

Yet with its form separated from the light of Elendil, this instrument can be possessed by the Dark Lord in order to deceive. Appropriately, Tolkien has Sauron in possession of the Ithil-stone, or Stone like the Moon, which again refers to the fickleness of worldly fortune. In his use of the palantír, the Dark Lord assumes a power in usurpation of the saintly authority of the Faithful in order to oppose them. Furthermore, by means of the palantíri, Sauron deceives Saruman in his tower of Orthanc. This tower was of Númenórean construction, formerly the dwelling place of "wise men that watched the stars,"[22] and a location for one of the Seeing-stones. "Orthanc" signifies both "forked height" and "cunning mind;" the name of the forked sword, Dhul-Fiqar, signifies the power of discrimination, and is depicted in Islamic mysticism as the "Sword of the Mind." Curiously, the Imam `Ali,

---

[22] "The Road to Isengard," *The Two Towers.*

wielder of Dhul-Fiqar, is also the patron of the star-watchers in Islam. In *The Lord of the Rings*, the fortress of Orthanc is recovered from the traitorous Saruman, whose cunning is humbled in a watery purification. The palantír of Orthanc is in turn wrested from the influence of the Dark Lord by the heir of Elendil. These developments depict remarkably well the susceptibility of symbols to inversion, as already seen in the example of Saruman, and moreover that their legitimacy may be restored only in the light of transcendence. In the absence of this light, the mind – even that of Saruman - is incapable of discriminating reality from parody. This is why the cosmological sciences, such as Astrology and Alchemy, if separated from the light of revelation, may mislead rather than guide.[23] Indeed the forging of the ring of the Dark Lord was itself the achievement of a magical science indebted to and then in rebellion against the Elven light of guidance. For the most part, Tolkien avoids associating goodness with "magical" operations belonging to the cosmological sciences.

Yet the foregoing should serve as evidence that *The Lord of the Rings* itself operates according to a rigorous science of symbols, and so is concerned with profound cosmic principles, whence it derives its "reality." Its "applicability" depends upon how transparent historical events are to these same principles. This imaginary history depicts very clearly power that is legitimate and luminous and opposed to its counterfeit, a tyranny whose talisman is the parody of a sacred symbol, specifically the Ring of Solomon. It is not too difficult to find examples of the inversion of symbols in history, with the swastika of the Third Reich being but an obvious example.[24] This problem of inversion must no doubt be accounted for in the search for "applicability;" for instance, those that would imagine the Eastern Enemy in Middle-earth to be an allegorical depiction of Islam as the enemy of Catholicism, must consider that in the Crusades, Catholicism conquered the Dome of the Rock – the "Temple of Solomon" – that became the stronghold of nine riders called Templars, Christians wielding swords both against Islam and the example of Jesus.

---

[23] Such was the case with Dr. Dee's notorious scrying experiments with Edward Kelley.

[24] The flags of Israel and the Turkish Republic are likewise examples.

3

The Light of Aman

Mention was made above to the eschatological Tradition of the believer's face shining "like a star." Some attention must be given to the very same image as it appears in Middle-earth, especially since the motif of a star shining from the brow seems to have had very great significance for Tolkien. Not only does he return to it again and again in *The Lord of the Rings*, but it is moreover the dominant theme of his last story, the very personal *Smith of Wootton Major*. This image may first be uncovered from the mythology of Middle-earth that precedes *The Lord of the Rings* and that is properly its foundation.

According to Tolkien, the "Blessed Realm" is an angelic domain far to the West of Middle-earth. Sometimes called Aman, it is from this place that the luminosity of the Elves originates, since those who have resided there are known as the "Light-elves." The light and glory of Aman was in the beginning divided and manifest in the form of two luminous trees. Because of the perishability of the trees, this light was afterwards preserved in the triad of mysterious jewels called the silmarilli, embodying apparently the complementary trees and their transcendent and single source. The symbol of the three jewels or luminaries is in Islam an emblem of the Sahib al-Qiran, or "Lord of the Fortunate Conjunction," and appeared in Ottoman art as the çintamani motif.[1] Tolkien has the two trees pass away, but from their fruits were made the sun and moon.[2] Always the Luciferian Melkor, master of Sauron, envied the silmarilli, and ultimately only one of the jewels was preserved against his evil. With the "light of heaven" in his face,

---

[1] This symbol was inherited by the Islamic world from China.
[2] Trees of the sun and of the moon are also alchemical symbols.

Eärendil the Mariner[3] bore the silmaril on his brow and became the first man to reach Aman, obtaining help against evil and mercy for both Men and Elves. The light of the jewel, and the man who bore it, was then raised to a luminous station, becoming a star of hope and of guidance in the Western sky.

It is this star that guides Men to Númenor. In keeping with alchemical symbolism, Tolkien has designed the emblem of Eärendil as a rayed formulation of the Seal of Solomon; yet Númenor, the "Land of the Star," is a pentagram in outline. Although this distinction seems to have been a source of confusion for the publishers of *The Lord of the Rings*,[4] it should instead be observed that this distinction demonstrates the subtlety of Tolkien's understanding, since the six points of the star in the sky and the five points of the land formation are in accordance with the "celestial" significance of the number six and the "terrestial" significance of the number five.[5] The legacy of this Star of Eärendil lives in two lines of descent:[6] on the brows of Eärendil's Elven sons, such as Elrond Halfelven of the White Council, and in the "Star of Elendil" diadem of the realm of Arnor, an heirloom of the Númenóreans whose ancestry is likewise traced to Eärendil. There should be little doubt that this Star of Elendil should be identified with the Seal of Solomon, since only the star of six points symbolizes the transcendence of Elendil's authority.

---

[3] Tolkien's first composition concerning Eärendil was in fact the first in his entire mythology; this was a poem, "The Voyage of Éarendel the Evening Star," inspired at a relative's farm, the name of which – "Phoenix Farm" – is of course significant in the context of Alchemy.

[4] This confusion is apparent when recent editions of *The Lord of the Rings* published after the passing of the author indiscriminately substituted a five-pointed for the six-pointed star in the index for motifs deriving from the Star of Eärendil.

[5] Cf. René Guénon, "Celestial Numbers & Terrestrial Numbers," *The Great Triad*. The pentagram of Númenor is in fact divided into six regions, with its central and supreme region dominated by the "Pillar of Heaven," and so the celestial significance of the sixth "point" is made clear. While on the subject of this number, it should not be forgotten that the dividing of *The Lord of the Rings* into three volumes was not the author's preference; in fact the story is comprised of six books.

[6] It should also be mentioned that the Phial of Galadriel that Frodo the Ring-bearer carries into the darkness of Sauron's realm was filled with the light of the Star of Eärendil.

All these forms of the "Light of Aman and the fate of Arda" must be seen to have a remarkable relationship to certain ideas in Islam. To begin with, the Elvish "Arda" appears synonymous with the Arabic "Ard," both signifying Earth. Yet Tolkien's meanings of "blessed" and "protected from evil" for the name "Aman" are in fact precisely those of the Arabic word; indeed Aman is a Divine Name.[7] In turn, the Prophet Muhammad was called "Amin," a related name signifying "faithful" or "trustworthy." In the mystical doctrine of the "Light of Muhammad," all of creation is held to proceed from his light. Its original form was the very best of created materials, a luminous jewel "brilliant as the sun and moon" that was first deposited on the forehead of Adam. All the Heavenly assembly glorified Adam for the sake of his shining brow, all except Satan, who envied the light that ennobled man above himself. This light was preserved from Satan's influence, however, and passed through the generations upon the brows of the descendents of Adam – among them the prophet Noah through the Flood - until the age of the Prophet Muhammad. Clearly the association of the mysterious silmaril[8] with the Light of Muhammad should not be lost sight of.

The journey of Eärendil to an angelic realm and his heavenly attainment recalls the fate of the prophet Elias, who became "human-angelic, earthly-heavenly." Now Tolkien admitted that the name Eärendil is in reality an Anglo-Saxon poetic expression for the star as herald, an expression that referred to John the Baptist as a divine messenger;[9] and John the Baptist is identified in the Bible with Elias, or rather an "Eliatic function."[10] Besides Elias, the prophet Idris is another form of the Thrice-Great Hermes who should be mentioned, since it is even more exactly the ascension of Idris that may be compared with the installation of Eärendil as a star. As already mentioned, Idris maintains in Islam a permanent position in connection with a heavenly luminary,

---

[7] It is significant that the Biblical Amen and the Egyptian Amon are both related to the Arabic word; however, their respective meanings are distinct from the Arabic. Interestingly, Tolkien employs the word Amon as the Elvish word for "hill."

[8] It should be noted that the mysterious substance from which the silmarilli were made is called silima, a word deriving from a root s-l-m, which happens to be the root of the Arabic word islam.

[9] *Letters*, number 297.

[10] Cf. Leo Schaya, "The Eliatic Function," *Studies in Comparative Religion*, Winter-Spring, 1999.

only in his case the luminary is not a star but the sun; and just as the sun is at the center of heavenly movement, so is Idris recognized in Islamic mysticism as the living Pole of the cosmos.[11] Yet in this role he is the deputy of the Light of Muhammad,[12] of which the sun as a source of light is but a sign. Of course, in the alchemical symbolism adopted by Tolkien, since the sun figures as one term in a cosmic pair, it is the star that here signifies the light of transcendence.[13] Of course, there is also among stars the Pole Star. In the chapter of the Holy Qur'an called "The Star," the Night Journey and Ascension of the Prophet of Islam through the angelic realm is recalled. Commentators recognize in the star of the Qur'an the Prophet himself, and "The Piercing Star" is one of his many names.

Another significant term relating to Aman is the Arabic word for faith, "iman," and so the stars of the Elven brows of the line of Eärendil can be seen as relating to the "light of iman" on the believer's face. Here it should be mentioned that in Islam, becoming a believer is more than calling oneself a Muslim, or "one who submits:" "Ye believe not, but rather say "We submit," for faith hath not yet entered into your hearts."[14] More accurately, the believer belongs to the ranks of saints. The special character of those whom Tolkien calls the Faithful of Númenor arises from their kinship with the People of the Stars. A scion of the lunar tree of Aman had been brought by the Faithful under Elendil's command to Middle-earth, and remained an heirloom and emblem of the Men of the West, that is, of Númenórean descent. In fact in an Islamic Tradition the believer is compared to a tree, and since white is moreover the color

---

[11] Chodkiewicz, *op. cit.*, pages 93-4. The swastika is a symbol of the cosmic Pole.

[12] Among the mysterious pronouncements of Taliesin, that most illustrious bard of ancient Britain, are the declarations: "I was patriarch to Elijah and Enoch... I was instructor to the whole universe." Such declarations are in keeping with the doctrine of the Light of Muhammad; in fact this association is all but confirmed by the meaning of his name, for "Taliesin" is really a title signifying "shining brow."

[13] This symbolism may be traced to the earliest formulations of Hermeticism; it was preserved by the Sabians into the Islamic era, and so came to be inherited by Latin Alchemy. It should be observed that Tolkien's linguistic element that signifies star – êl – clearly recalls the same element that signifies divinity in languages of the ancient Near East.

[14] *Qur'an* XLIX, 14

traditionally worn by believers, this tree is a very remarkable emblem belonging to "the Faithful."

Yet another word with the same root should be mentioned: "amanat," a word signifying an inherited and sacred "trust" and relating especially to the heirlooms of prophets. In the world of Islam, the caliph was literally the Prophet's "representative," who therefore inherited a treasury of relics called the "Amanat al-Muqaddas," or "Holy Trust." This custom may be understood in light of the following verse of the Holy Qur'an:

> And their prophet said unto them: Lo! the sign of his kingdom is that there shall come unto you the Ark of the Covenant wherein is Sakinah from your Lord, and a remnant of that which the house of Moses and the house of Aaron left behind, the angels bearing it. Lo! herein shall be a sign for you if you are faithful.[15]

So in Islam, the sign of the legitimacy of worldly power – the "kingdom" - was the inheritance of the relics of prophets. Qur'anic commentators provide various descriptions of the contents of the Ark, but it is significant in the context of *The Lord of the Rings* that the Staffs of Moses and Aaron, and even the Ring of Solomon, have been included. But an even greater significance may be found in the history of the Ark of the Covenant in Islam. Together with the Black Stone of Mecca, it is a treasure from Paradise according to Islamic sources. Containing images of all the prophets who would descend from Adam, it became an heirloom passed from generation to generation. This, of course, recalls the tradition mentioned above concerning the descent of the Light of Muhammad. Indeed these two inheritances were long together, with the Ark even containing, among its other relics, the record of the oath sworn by the custodians of the Light to guard its sanctity.[16] However, in the time of the prophet Abraham, these two inheritances were divided between his sons: the line of prophets from Isaac – those of the Jews – would preserve the Ark and its contents, while the highest Arab nobility from the line of Ishmael would receive the Light of Muhammad.

---

[15] II, 248.

[16] Cf. Hajjah Amina Adil, *Muhammad, the Messenger of Islam: His Life and Prophecy,* Islamic Supreme Council of America, 2002.

Certainly the heirlooms of the kingdom of the Men of the West are afforded great importance in Tolkien's vision. As a repository for the heirlooms of the Faithful, the house of Elrond is an Ark. The name Elrond is related to Tolkien's word for "cave" or "dome," and Elrond preserves what Tolkien calls "the ancient wisdom."[17] "Rivendell" signifies a deep valley and therefore a sheltered container: "'There's something of everything here, if you understand me: the Shire and the Golden Wood and Gondor and kings' houses and inns and meadows and mountains all mixed.'"[18] The drowning of the Ringwraiths at the Ford of Rivendell in *The Fellowship of the Ring* is a variant of the "ordeal of the river" that discriminates the faithful from unbelievers, mentioned in the verse of the Holy Qur'an that immediately follows the verse concerning the Ark, and concludes: "How many a little company hath overcome a mighty host by Allah's leave! Allah is with the steadfast."[19] Clearly there is a relationship between the contents of the Ark and the heirlooms preserved in Rivendell, especially the sceptre (synonymous with a staff of authority) and the ring. The form of this Ring of Barahir also relates symbolically to the caduceus: "like to twin serpents, whose eyes were emeralds, and their heads met beneath a crown of golden flowers, that the one upheld and the other devoured."[20] Yet most remarkably, the primary heirlooms, the Sword and Star of Elendil, have a very particularly "Muhammadan" significance.

Confirming this association of the Númenórean heirlooms and the contents of the Ark of the Covenant is Tolkien's comparison of the destroyed temple of Númenor with the Temple of the Ark;[21] so the ships of the Faithful that escaped relate both to the Ark of Noah and the Ark of the Covenant. The destruction of the Temple in Jerusalem announced a change in history, and this surely is the general significance of the fall of Númenor. More particularly, the Temple's destruction may be

---

[17] *Letters*, number 131. It should be noted that the Elvish name for Rivendell, Imladris, contains the name Idris, the most ancient form of the Thrice-great Hermes.

[18] "Many Partings," *The Return of the King*.

[19] II, 249. It is even remarkable that supernatural horses appear in the river that overwhelms the Ringwraiths, since Islamic sources relate that Solomon kept "water-horses" in his stables at the Temple that housed the Ark.

[20] "Of Beren and Lúthien," *The Silmarillion*. "Flowers of gold" is an expression in the language of Alchemy.

[21] *Letters*, number 156.

understood in relation to the development of Christianity, whereas the historical loss of the Ark of the Covenant contrasts with the embodiment of the Light of Muhammad in the Prophet of Islam. However, the Sakinah mentioned in the above verse was not lost; whereas the Sakinah had been externally manifested with the Ark of the Covenant, the Sufis of Islam understand that with the appearance of the Prophet Muhammad, the Sakinah thereafter descends upon the hearts of believers,[22] a consequence of the role of saints in Islam as "the heirs of prophets." There is also a Tradition reporting that in the time of the Prophet Muhammad a chest containing the images of all the prophets was in the possession of the Emperor of East Rome.[23] So the empire of Rome, entrusted with this record of the physiognomy of the prophets, inherited likewise the responsibility of recognizing the significance of the Prophet of Islam, in whom the two legacies of Abraham – the Light of Muhammad and what is contained in the Ark - are reunited. Certainly for the Ottoman caliphs, the relics of the Prophet Muhammad had replaced the heirlooms of the other prophets as the "sign" of their "kingdom."

In Middle-earth, the heirs of Elendil each in turn receives his sword as the sign of their investiture, and each Ottoman caliph in succeeding to the Amanat was likewise invested with a sword, a sword decorated with a verse naming the Sakinah and with serpentine quillons – and the eyes of these twin serpents are likewise emeralds. It should also not be overlooked that the heirs of Elendil are by right the kings or commanders of the Elendili or Faithful, and that the most renowned title of the caliph or representative of the Prophet is Amir al-Mu'minin, the Commander of the Faithful.

---

[22] Chodkiewicz, *op. cit.*, page 73.
[23] Cf. "Le Coffre d'Héraclius et la Tradition du 'Tâbût' Adamique" in Michel Vâlsan's *L'Islam et la Fonction de René Guénon*. Similar images were reported to be in the possession of the Emperor of China.

4

The Western Sun

It may seem strange that the light in Middle-earth is associated with the West, and not the East that is customarily associated with illumination. Only the Dúnedain, literally the Men of the West, are not estranged from the People of the Stars. In the return of the king of the Dúnedain, the luminous quality of the West is evoked time after time; thus Elendil's Sword Reforged is called "flame" or "light" of the West or "direction of the sun." In Islamic Traditions also, the West becomes the location of light, for the "Sun rising in the West" is yet another sign of eschatology. The power to reverse the natural course of the sun in the western sky has been demonstrated in traditional accounts of the prophets Joshua - successor of Moses as inheritor of the Ark of the Covenant - Solomon, and Muhammad; this miracle shared by prophets manifests the transcendence of their authority.[1] Yet the appearance of such a transcendent authority at the end of the world suggests that the prophecy of the "Sun rising in the West" refers to the appearance of a descendent of the Prophet Muhammad known as Muhammad al-Mahdi, the Caliph of God whose enemy is the Dajjal.[2]

> All that is gold does not glitter,
> Not all those who wander are lost;
> The old that is strong does not wither,
> Deep roots are not reached by the frost.

---

[1] It would seem that the creatures called Ents and Huorns belong purely to Tolkien's imagination, so it is very remarkable that another sign of the transcendent authority of the Prophet of Islam in the Traditions is the moving, walking, and speaking of trees in confirmation of his prophethood (Qadi `Iyad, op. cit., pages 165-8). What is more, another Tradition relates that trees endowed with speech will give help to the faithful on an eschatological battlefield.

[2] The alchemist Jabir Ibn Hayyan shared this interpretation.

> From the ashes a fire shall be woken,
>   A light from the shadows shall spring;
> Renewed shall be blade that was broken:
>   The crownless again shall be king.[3]

Indeed many are the similarities between the Caliph of God and the "prophesied" king of these verses. Aragorn, owner of the Sword Reforged, is known as "Hope" and the "Renewer" and is identified in the phrase, "Not all those who wander are lost;" that is to say he is "guided." "Al-Mahdi" literally means the "Guided;" he is the hoped-for leader brought forth with "the sword and noble character" who manifests, with a name identical to that of the Prophet of Islam, a renewed appearance of the reality of Muhammad. This relates to what is said in the traditions of Islamic chivalry, "The First is like the Last and the Last is like the First."[4] Tolkien asserts that Aragorn was "yet more like to Elendil than any before him,"[5] and both the heir of Elendil and the descendent of the Prophet belong to the fortieth generation in their lines of descent. Aragorn is the Hobbits', and so also the reader's, guide to Rivendell, and it is related in Tradition that al-Mahdi is so called because he is guided to the Ark of the Covenant. The Traditions also relate that "he will fill the earth will equity and justice as it was filled with oppression and tyranny," and here the Arabic word for tyranny literally signifies "shadow;" remarkably, the influence of the Dark Lord is identified by precisely the same image throughout Tolkien's writings. But perhaps most significant, in light of the Star of Elendil diadem and the "white flame" seen flickering on Aragorn's brow by Elven eyes[6], is that a most distinguishing mark of the Mahdi's physiognomy in the Traditions is that his forehead shines "like a glittering star."[7]

---

[3] "Strider," *The Fellowship of the Ring*.

[4] *The Royal Book of Spiritual Chivalry*, page 26.

[5] "Of the Rings of Power and the Third Age," *The Silmarillion*.

[6] "The Riders of Rohan," *The Two Towers*. It is with the flaming nimbus – another example of fire in its luminous aspect - that the Light of Muhammad is depicted in Islamic miniature painting.

[7] On the other hand, the forehead of the Dajjal is described as marked with the word "disbeliever." It is intriguing, then, to recall the Jewish legend of the Golem with its marked forehead, since in *The Lord of the Rings* Gollum is the name of the servant of the Enemy's One Ring.

Yet all these correspondences might be dismissed were it not for the events recounted in *The Return of the King*. Indeed before then the Star of Elendil does not appear. Mention was made above to the preparation of the "lunar" or "passive" aspect in the alchemical work. In the first two volumes of *The Lord of the Rings*, Aragorn appears in a relatively passive role, serving first the Ring-bearer and then the King Théoden of Rohan in the battle against the armies of Saruman. A change in his character becomes manifest upon his restoration of the Seeing-stone of Orthanc, when Aragorn shows himself to the Dark Lord:

> ...he saw me, but in other guise than you see me here...To know that I lived and walked the earth was a blow to his heart, I deem; for he knew it not till now. The eyes in Orthanc did not see through the armour of Théoden; but Sauron has not forgotten Isildur and the sword of Elendil. Now in the very hour of his great designs the heir of Isildur and the Sword are revealed; for I showed the blade re-forged to him.[8]

This "revelation" announces a different phase of the alchemical process that may rightly be termed active, and therefore "solar." The distinction between these phases is exemplified in the manner in which Aragorn enters into the necessary "extinction:" through the "tomb" of Moria, he is a passive follower; but with the opening of *The Return of the King*, he must lead on the "Paths of the Dead."

A company of Dúnedain called Rangers, riding with the Elven sons of Elrond from the North, unexpectedly arrives to join Aragorn their chief for his journey to Minas Anor, renamed Minas Tirith. Against his desire, he is compelled to travel first under the earth on the "Paths of the Dead." Here the "Dead" actually refers to men cursed for having failed to fight against the Enemy after their oath of allegiance to Isildur, indeed they had formerly worshipped Sauron. So Aragorn, the heir of Isildur, summons these "oathbreakers" again to the "Stone of Erech," a black stone believed to have "fallen from the sky" and preserved through the flood of Atalantë, so that they might fulfill their oath and "have peace." With the unfurling of the black banner received from Elrond's daughter, his betrothed, he is then able to proceed to the city of Minas Tirith.

---

[8] "The Passing of the Grey Company," *The Return of the King*.

Here the identification of Aragorn as an image of the Mahdi reveals this "history" as a very close image of the eschatological events surrounding the latter's appearance, for in the Traditions of Islam, it is at the Black Stone of Islam – and Islam is literally "to have peace" - that the Mahdi first receives oaths of allegiance. Of course, it should be remembered that the real Black Stone is believed to be from Paradise. Before its placement in the Holy Ka`ba, the temple built by Abraham in Arabia,[9] this Stone had been preserved from the Flood in the time of Noah within a mountain once called al-Amin for that reason. Indeed the Black Stone is regarded as the "Stone of Amanat" because it is held to contain a record of a primordial oath, an oath referred to in the following verses: "Did I not charge you, O ye sons of Adam, that ye worship not Satan-Lo! He is your clear foe! But that ye worship Me? That was the right path."[10] So the Black Stone is the gathering place of those seeking to reaffirm this oath in the ritual of the pilgrimage.

In another verse of the Holy Qur'an, the oath of allegiance to a Heavenly representative is described: "Lo! Those who swear allegiance unto thee, swear allegiance only unto Allah. The hand of Allah is above their hands. So whosoever breaketh his oath, breaketh it only to his soul's hurt; while whosoever keepeth his covenant with Allah, on him will He bestow an immense reward."[11] The discrimination between the oath to worship God and the worship of the Enemy of men is especially significant here, for the one-eyed enemy of the Mahdi is, like Sauron, worshipped by his followers.

The details of Tolkien's description only make this identification more certain. For instance, it is even part of the Traditions that the Mahdi receives the allegiances at the Black Stone somewhat against his desire. In addition, the company between thirty and forty in number that joins Aragorn from the North before the gathering at the black stone suggests

---

[9] The history of at-Tabari relates that the Sakinah directed Abraham in its construction. At-Tabari's sources describe the Sakinah alternately as a "gale-force wind with two heads" that positioned itself "the way a snake coils," as having "two wings and a head like that of a snake," and as having the power of speech (Volume II: *Prophets and Patriarchs*, translated by Brinner, SUNY, 1987, pages 70-1). These strange images recall the "winged serpent" that John Michell associates with the Hermeticism of Atlantis (*The New View Over Atlantis*, Harper & Row, 1983).

[10] *Qur'an* XXXVI, 60-1

[11] *Ibid.* XLVIII, 10

the saints known as Abdal who are said to reach the Mahdi from Sham – literally the "North" from the real Black Stone – especially since the Abdal are usually forty, although the number thirty also appears in the Traditions.[12] And as if it must be so, the banner unfurled in Tolkien's vision is black, with its emblems hidden, even though Tolkien is otherwise quite consistent in having white stand against the darkness of evil; for the Mahdi appears in the Traditions with the Banner of the Prophet that is black.

This Noble Banner signaled the very presence of the Prophet of Islam. Originally named the Eagle, it was made from the black woolen fabric of the wife of the Prophet, so even the association of Aragorn's black banner with his betrothed is significant. The Black Banner was a most distinguishing mark of the Amanat of the caliph, and was housed alongside the other relics unless carried to the battlefield against the enemies of the heirs of Muhammad. Very like the Ark of the Covenant with its Sakinah within that had formerly brought victory on the battlefield, so this relic of the Prophet was revered on campaign. There the lords of the Prophet's Family surrounded it, and the chapter of Victory from the Holy Qur'an was recited that contains references to the Sakinah. In Middle-earth, the black banner appears among the Elven lords who ride with it from Rivendell to the battlefield. Furthermore, under the Ottoman caliphs, the Ghuraba' was a mounted guard of the Noble Banner on campaign, and their designation carried the significance of both "strangers" and "western;"[13] and it is the "Rangers" of the Men of the West who, having become "strangers" in Middle-earth, appear here as the custodians of the banner. Their only insignia – or rather talisman - that of the "rayed star," the Rangers moreover are mounted with "spear and bow and sword," that is, precisely the weaponry of Ottoman cavalry, or rather a cavalry of traditional Islam; indeed the bow, while being the Muhammadan weapon *par excellence*, was never held in honor by the chivalry of Christendom.[14]

---

[12] Cf. on this subject "The Immense Merits of al-Sham" in *Islamic Doctrines & Beliefs, Volume 1*.

[13] "Blessed are the strangers" appears in a Tradition relating to the end of time.

[14] In fact, in Tolkien's vision, the bow is the distinctive weapon of the Elves, whereas in Islam, the bow is the weapon of angels who instructed the prophets in its proper use. It may further be observed that the bow's form, with upper and lower limbs united at the grip, itself symbolizes the uniting of dualities. Cf.

The estrangement of the Men of the West in Middle-earth suggests another aspect of eschatology, that the appearance of the light of the West follows a period of injustice, ignorance, and occultation. The gray raiment of the Rangers, like the gray robes which veil for a while Gandalf the White, contributes to their unobtrusiveness during this period. The reader is first told of the Rangers that they "were believed to have strange powers of sight and hearing, and to understand the languages of beasts and birds."[15] While Tolkien already included the "language of the birds" as a motif in *The Hobbit*, it should moreover be observed that this mysterious language remarkably appears both in Nordic legend and in the Holy Qur'an, and is identified in the latter as belonging to the knowledge of prophets.[16] Such knowledge is appropriate, then, for saints, who are in Islam the heirs of prophets. Furthermore, in the context of sainthood in Islam, "powers of sight and hearing" recall the following Sacred Tradition, in which God relates of the worshipper: "When I love him, I am his hearing with which he hears, his sight by which he sees, his hand with which he acts, and his foot with which he walks."[17] The role of the Rangers is also described in a way that demands a lengthier quote:

> "Peace and freedom...The North would have known them little but for us. Fear would have destroyed them. But when dark things come from the houseless hills, or creep from sunless woods, they fly from us. What roads would any dare to tread, what safety would there be in quiet lands, or in the homes of simple men at night, if the Dúnedain were asleep, or were all gone into the grave?...Travelers scowl at us, and countrymen give us scornful names. 'Strider' I am to one fat man who lives within a day's march of foes that would freeze his heart, or lay his little town in ruin, if he were not guarded ceaselessly. Yet we would not want it otherwise. If simple folk are free from care and fear, simple they will be, and we must

---

Ananda K. Coomaraswamy, "The Symbolism of Archery," *Ars Islamica*, X, 1943, pages 104-19.

[15] "At the Sign of the Prancing Pony," *The Fellowship of the Ring.*

[16] XXVII, 15.

[17] It should be noted that Aragorn the Ranger possesses "strange powers" not only in "sight and hearing," but also in his hands which "bring healing" and his feet, for which he is called "Strider" and "Wingfoot," and so in each of the dimensions included in this Sacred Tradition.

be secret to keep them so. That has been the task of my kindred...But now the world is changing once again. A new hour comes..."[18]

Such a role may be compared with the description of a high rank of sainthood in the teachings of Islamic mysticism:

> They are knights...the princes and leaders of the people of the Way of God...They are the wise ones who put every thing in its proper place...They are not known for doing extraordinary things, nor are they considered important...They are the hidden ones, the free, the guardians of the world, concealed amongst mankind.[19]

With the coming of a new hour, these Rangers appear with Aragorn, their chief; this appearance, as well as their emergence from the underground path the Dúnedain must take, echoes the belief in the hiddenness of the saintly hierarchy before its appearance with the Mahdi.

According to Tolkien, the conflict in *The Lord of the Rings* "is about God, and His sole right to divine honour;"[20] in this conflict, "the Númenóreans (and Elves) were absolute monotheists."[21] Tolkien's biographer has asserted that the religious beliefs of Middle-earth are not explicitly Christian so as not to deprive them of "imaginative color," and concludes: "So while God is present in Tolkien's universe, He remains unseen."[22] Yet it is such "absolute monotheism" that accords so well with Islam; surely it is not for "imaginative color" that Tolkien chooses a black stone[23] as the location for his oath of monotheism. According to the

---

[18] "The Council of Elrond," *The Fellowship of the Ring*.
[19] Quoted in Stephen Hirtenstein, *The Unlimited Mercifier*, Anqa/White Cloud, 1999, pages 104, 136.
[20] *Letters*, number 183.
[21] *Ibid.*, number 192 (note).
[22] Carpenter, *op.cit.*, page 99.
[23] Some incidental remarks may be made concerning the name Erech. Tolkien himself responded to the question of whether the Biblical Erech in Mesopotamia was his model, and while admitting that he knew "a good deal about Mesopotamia," he denied the importance of the city to *The Lord of the Rings* (*Letters*, number 297). Nevertheless, since the Stone of Erech was established by the Númenórean Faithful, it is interesting to note that the building of that ancient

monotheism of Islam, allegiance is "only unto Allah," yet proceeds in accordance with the order to "Obey God, the Messenger, and those among you in command."[24] Whereas the "oathbreakers" are those who are "dead" though their disobedience to the Men of the West and so to God, the loyal Rangers exemplify the faithful mentioned in the Holy Qur'an: "Of the believers are Men who are true to that which they covenanted with Allah." These Men are further described as having "not altered in the least,"[25] and the Rangers, compared to whom the knights of Rohan "'look almost as boys,'"[26] had never failed their commander. And so these Men of the West ultimately recall another Tradition of the Prophet Muhammad: "The people of the West shall not cease to be victorious, standing for Truth, until the hour rises."[27]

Mesopotamian city is associated with "Seven Sages" who "lived before the Flood" (Hancock and Bauval, *op. cit.*, page 201). And Erech also happens to be the same as the ancient pagan city of Uruk, a name Tolkien uses for the Orcs. Finally, its modern Arabic name of Warka recalls the Christian companion of Muhammad named Waraka, whose confirmation of Muhammad's prophethood corresponds in some measure to the confirmation of Jesus by the Three Wise Men. The expression of Waraka's accord with the "absolute monotheism" of the Prophet of Islam took place, significantly, near the Black Stone at Mecca.

[24] *Qur'an* IV, 59.

[25] *Ibid.* XXXIII, 23.

[26] "The Passing of the Grey Company."

[27] Quoted in *Islamic Doctrines & Beliefs, Volume 1*, page 128.

5

The City

There is in Tolkien's White Mountains[1] a chain of seven "beacon-hills," upon which signal fires are positioned. Now, the beacon-hill most distant from Minas Tirith is called Halifirien, and a recent study of *The Lord of the Rings* states, "this must be Old English halig fyrgen, 'Holy Mountain.' But we never find out who or what it was once holy to."[2] However, in a posthumously published essay written after *The Lord of the Rings*, Tolkien himself has identified this "holy mountain" as the former tomb of Elendil, and what is more, gives its former name: the Hill of Anwar.[3] This identification is remarkable indeed, since "anwar" is very

---

[1] René Guénon in *Le Roi du Monde* mentions White Mountain as a designation of a spiritual center. Since he also mentions the many forms of the name Thule which have more especially designated spiritual centers, it is of interest to note that in appendix E of *The Lord of the Rings*, Tolkien translates thúle from Elvish as "spirit." Remarkably, the Germanic Thule society seems to have been linked in its formation to Islamic mysticism, and in particular the Bektashi Sufi Order, through the Ottoman Rosicrucian Baron Rudolf von Sebottendorf; unfortunately, "the Pan-European spiritual outlook of Sebottendorf and Thule was distorted by Hitler and the Nazis into a bloody Germanic chauvinism" (M. Sabeheddin, "Hitler, Nazis & the Occult," *New Dawn*, number 41, March-April 1997). This last insight may be compared with Tolkien's own view: "I have...a burning private grudge against that ruddy little ignoramous Adolf Hitler for ruining, perverting, misapplying, and making for ever accursed, that noble northern spirit, a supreme contribution to Europe, which I have ever loved, and tried to present in its true light" (Quoted in Carpenter, *op. cit.*, page 197). Here the "applicability" of Tolkien's vision to his own time becomes rather more profound than is generally understood; his rise of a Western Sun provided a "true light" to dispel the sinister parody of Hitler and his swastika.

[2] T.A. Shippey, *J.R.R. Tolkien: Author of the Century*, page 175.

[3] "Cirion and Eorl" and "The Tradition of Isildur," *Unfinished Tales*.

simply the Arabic name for "lights," a name which moreover confirms what has already been said to associate Elendil with the example of the prophets in Islam. The Prophet Muhammad is in particular associated with the Hill of Light (singular), upon which he first received the revelation of the Holy Qur'an. In a sense, anwar literally refers to the lights of the star, associated with Elendil, and the sun and moon that proceed from him, both in his sword and in his sons. Tolkien identifies the Hill of Anwar as the original "mid-point" or center of Gondor, and a site of sacred oath-taking and royal initiation. The transference of the body of Elendil from its hidden tomb on the Hill of Anwar to Minas Tirith signifies at once a sanctification of the city in recompense for the loss of its line of kings, but also a preparation for the city to serve as a new center upon the outward return of the lights of Elendil in the person of his long hidden heir. Still, the Hill of Anwar was later known as Holy Mountain since it retained some sanctity from its former function as the resting place of Elendil.

The city of Minas Tirith is located at the foot of the White Mountains.[4] In his letters, Tolkien has confirmed the relation of the city of Minas Tirith to Rome, both Rome proper and East Rome, that is Constantinople.[5] Both cities are expressions of empire, of a universal kingdom by divine right, the cornerstone of which is the emperor himself. In ancient Rome, the royal power of the emperor had been united to sacred authority. Christian Rome preserved the imperial function, despite the absence of royal power from the historical role of Jesus. Indeed East Rome, the city of Constantine, preserved from its foundation a tradition of Empire in the service of Christianity, whereas the imperial tradition in the city of Rome had fallen in the Dark Ages. When the papacy sought in the Middle Ages to reestablish an empire from Rome, both the new Holy Roman Emperors and the papacy with

---

[4] More exactly, the city is at the foot of Mount Mindolluin, the name of which refers to the color blue and so to the mountain's role as a link between the earth and sky. There is moreover a tradition in Islam that the color of the sky is itself a reflection from the mountain located at the meeting place of Heaven and Earth.

[5] "Middle-earth," of course, is simply a variant of "Mediterranean." At the same time, Tolkien specifically offered that Minas Tirith "is at about the latitude of Florence" (Letters, number 294). Florence was the center of Hermetic study in Europe during the Renaissance.

imperial pretensions claimed the same function, a function that does not belong to Christianity.

The symbolism so far considered that expresses in a general sense the union of the heavenly and earthly, such as the Seal of Solomon, must also include the more particular union of heavenly authority and earthly power in government. Tolkien presents this particular union in Elendil, whose sanctity and power are symbolized by the two lights of the sun and moon, with worldly power being properly receptive or "lunar" in relation to heavenly authority. Yet it should not be overlooked that Elendil himself is identified with the star, and so stands above such distinctions.[6] The union of sanctity and power is also to some degree perpetuated in Elendil's house of "lineal priest kings," as Tolkien called them.[7] In *The Lord of the Rings*, this union is expressed in the phrase, "the hands of the king are the hands of a healer."[8] Healing, of course, is for the Christian world the best proof of sanctity, since healing was a specialty of Jesus. It is moreover said of the heir of Elendil:

> A great lord is that, and a healer; and it is a thing passing strange to me that the healing hand should also wield a sword. It is not thus in Gondor now, though once it was so, if old tales be true.[9]

This unity is indeed "strange" for a Christian like Tolkien, since the historical Jesus Christ was a healer and did not wield a sword. Historically, this was, however, the example of the Prophet of Islam and his caliphs. The first caliph of the Prophet Muhammad was his best friend Abu Bakr as-Siddiq, with whom he made his journey from Mecca to establish the "Luminous City" (Madina al-Munawwara); this event – the Hijra - marks the beginning of a new era in Islam. Following the example of the Prophet, the rule of his first representative from that city preserved the union of heavenly authority and royal power. It is significant that the title "as-Siddiq," meaning "the Truthful," is bestowed

---

6 Elendil and his sons correspond in some measure to the three functions discussed by Guénon in *Le Roi du Monde*, as well as to the Pole, the Imam of the Left, and the Imam of the Right in the saintly hierarchy of Islamic mysticism.

7 *Letters*, number 156.

8 "The Houses of Healing," *The Return of the King*. It is above all the Elves who possess great skill in healing

9 "The Steward and the King," *The Return of the King*.

also on the prophet Idris in the Holy Qur'an,[10] for Idris is also a "representative" of Muhammad in his solar station at the center or pole of the Heavenly spheres. The rule of such a representative on Earth embodies the Heavenly order, and may therefore be called a "Kingdom of Heaven on Earth."[11]

In Islamic angelology, the solar domain of Idris is associated with the Ruh or Spirit that is more particularly known as Mitatrun or Metatron. This name appears especially in a talismanic context, for example on the Ottoman "talismanic shirts" worn in battle. Baron Hammer-Purgstall, in his study of one such shirt, has identified Mitatrun with Mithra.[12] This identification is not arbitrary, since Mithra is especially associated with the light of the sun, and was known to the Romans as Mithras and Sol Invictus. The name Mithras numerically corresponds to 365, the number of days in the solar year; in the Bible, Enoch who is Idris is mentioned as living 365 years on Earth. Now the Persian cult of Mithra became the dominant cult of the military throughout the Roman Empire before its conversion to Christianity; indeed, the cult was well established in Britain by Roman troops. It has even been maintained that the legends of King Arthur, historically linked to the preservation of Roman order in Britain against barbarism, are in their foundations indebted to the cult of Mithras: so the wizard Merlin may be compared with Mithras, and the chivalry of the Round Table with the Mithraic ideals of a knightly brotherhood.[13] This discernment of Mithraic elements in Christian Britain provides but a glimpse of the profound importance of Mithraism in the Romanization of Christianity. Since it provided a royal initiation and so a knightly brotherhood for the Roman soldier, Mithraism was not easily eradicated by its Christian rivals; the new revelation did not include a form of royal initiation to naturally supplant the cult of Mithras. Already it has been established that Tolkien evokes Mithraism in Mithrandir,[14] a fact that could not

---

[10] XIX, 56-7.

[11] Another example is that of Joseph in Egypt, likewise called "as-Siddiq" in the Holy Qur'an, whose rule is presaged in astrological terms (cf. XII).

[12] *Journal asiatique*, volume IX, 1832.

[13] Cf. Sir Jehangir Coyagee, *The Legend of the Holy Grail: Its Iranian and Indian Analogues*, 1939.

[14] It should rather be said that Tolkien evokes Mitatrun, since Mithrandir's origin as one of the Maiar belongs especially to Tolkien's "angelology." However, it is rather Manwë, the King of Arda and Lord of the Valar who sends Mithrandir to

easily be explained away by those seeking a Christian interpretation of his work. Be that as it may, the ideal of a knightly brotherhood or fellowship is paramount in Tolkien's vision, and he moreover evokes rituals of royal initiation more than once in *The Lord of the Rings*.

With the end of Roman paganism, and in the absence of a sacred royalty from the Christian revelation, it is not surprising that Christendom should find inspiration in the royal traditions of the caliphs of Islam. Indeed, caliphal iconography was adopted by the Holy Roman Emperor in his claim to authority, and reached its fullest development in the rule of Frederick II. This process is comparable to the development of Christian knightly orders, claiming a function both sacred and royal, in response to and in imitation of the way of spiritual chivalry (futuwwah) in Islam. Futuwwah was in turn patterned on the example of the Prophet and his Companions, and reached its formulaic expression in the service of the caliphs.[15] In medieval Spain, where Christians sometimes even fought alongside Muslims, the swords of Christian knights even bore Latin translations of Qur'anic formulas. In the Ottoman Empire, the traditions of spiritual chivalry were embodied above all in the Janissary infantry bodyguard; and so Janissary bodyguards came to be adopted by

---

Middle-earth, who more closely resembles the spirit of Mitatrun; and in fact Tolkien admits Mithrandir's resemblance to the King of Arda: "it was believed by many of the 'Faithful' of that time that 'Gandalf' was the last appearance of Manwë himself" ("The Istari," *Unfinished Tales*). Now Manwë is clearly related to the name Manu (Celtic Menw), whose mythic function as "King of the World" René Guénon relates to Mitatrun (cf. *Le Roi du Monde*). Manwë is also Súlimo, "Lord of the Winds;" and as with the Elvish thúle (spirit) that becomes sûl (wind), "wind" and "spirit" are closely related in the Semitic languages. For that matter, the letters s-l-m refer to peace (salam), and so also to Solomon (whose relationship with Mitatrun has been noted in Esɪn, *op. cit.*, page 109 note 41). What is more, "peace" also relates to the Sakinah, usually translated as tranquility, whose residence was in the Temple of Solomon, and who brings help as a wind, as mentioned above. Yet Manwë's intercessionary aspect belongs rather to his luminous consort Elbereth, whose help is invoked by the Ring-bearer. That Melkor (Morgoth) is the brother of Manwë is in accord with the angelology relating to Mitatrun presented by Guénon, in particular concerning Mikaël and his shadow Samaël. This last point concerns the relationship of the solar archangel Michael to Mitatrun, as the luminous representative of the latter.

[15] Cf. the introduction to *The Royal Book of Spiritual Chivalry*. The shared heraldic use of the Hermetic black, white, and red – colors corresponding to the stages of the alchemical work – should also be mentioned.

Christian kings, most notably by Sobieski, a commander of armies against the Ottomans at Vienna. Despite theological opposition, and with the royal dimension absent from the Christian revelation, the influence of Islam in this realm was dominant. All this concerns the natural "passivity" of earthly or royal power in relation to revelation, and so corresponds to the imprinting of the Hermetic sciences by Islam; indeed Alchemy is called the "royal art."

The existence of the chest belonging to the Roman emperor that held the images of all the prophets suggests that the imperial function depended less upon Christianity than upon an historical succession of prophetic revelation. When the Ottoman armies of Islam conquered Constantinople at the end of the Middle Ages, the city was renewed in a real Renaissance. At the meeting of two continents and of two seas, Constantinople retained not only its name but also its imperial cornerstone in the person of the Ottoman ruler, and its imperial traditions succeeded naturally to the service of the religion of the Seal of all the prophets. In the Ottoman renovation of East Rome to an even greater glory, it could be said, as Tolkien relates of Minas Tirith, that "the City was made more fair than it had ever been, even in the days of its first glory...and after the ending of the Third Age of the world into the new age it preserved the memory and the glory of the years that were gone."[16] Even the symbol of the new sovereignty, the crescent surmounted by the star, is a synthesis of Byzantine and Ottoman iconography.

Similarly, a lunar symbol is united with stars on the black banner Aragorn brings to the renewal of Minas Tirith. These emblems belong originally to Elendil: the lunar Tree of Aman that stands for Gondor and the seven stars of his house. As mentioned above, seven stars were particularly associated in Islam with the Companions of the Cave, who are linked not only to the symbolism of the ship, but who were also the patron saints of sailors in Ottoman times. These significations are present as the stars appear on the ship that bears Aragorn and his companions to the city, after their emergence from the cavern of the Paths of the Dead. There is moreover an interesting correspondence between the approach of Aragorn to Minas Tirith and

---

[16] "The Steward and the King." As if to suggest this association, Tolkien has the enemies of Minas Tirith call the man of Gondor "tark," hardly distinguishable from the degraded word "Turk."

the investiture ceremony of the Ottoman caliphs of Constantinople: as part of his investiture with the sword, the Ottoman Lord of the Lands and Seas alternatively rode both on horseback and by boat, and the Owner of the Sword Reforged proceeds likewise in his rise to authority. The return of the stars of the Faithful to the city of Minas Tirith, like the transformation of Constantinople under the Ottomans, may be seen both as a conquest and as a restoration in accord with a "new age." Although the latter aspect certainly dominates Tolkien's vision, the former is not absent; for in the appearance of Aragorn, the Steward of the City perceives and finds only the end of his own sovereignty in fire and doom.[17]

While the conquest of Rome had been promised in the Traditions of the Prophet of Islam, and it became the honor of the Ottomans to renew East Rome, a further expectation related to Rome itself. In a sense both cities, although separated geographically, represent one reality, namely a center of Empire. The conquest of Constantinople by Islam represents its historical inheritance of that Imperial center, and so is distinguished from the conquest of Rome, which was extended into an eschatological hope; so it was for the Mahdi to conquer the great City. Strangely, this expectation, called the "Prophecy of the Red Apple," has been shown to relate to the Turkish word "nar."[18] Again, Tolkien evokes the Arabic meaning of this word, giving it a very great importance in his alchemical work; it is from this word that Tolkien derives not only Anárion and Narsil, but most significantly the proper name of the "Tower of the (western) Sun," Minas Anor. Since nar also signifies the pomegranate and therefore the city of Granada, the reconquest of that last stronghold of Islam in Spain became an eschatological hope of Western Islam. So this "prophecy" also signifies a reconquest.

Tolkien's description of Minas Tirith very carefully traces its structure. Still, while both Rome and East Rome are situated on sites having seven hills, it is by no means clear why either Rome should be recalled by its particular configuration of walls. There is, however, a very

---

[17] While the motif of Aragorn's black sails marking the end of another's sovereignty has been rightly related to the myth of Theseus' return, it should be recalled that the renowned alchemist Nicolas Flamel likewise employed this myth to describe the alchemical process.

[18] Cf. Hasluck, *Christianity and Islam Under the Sultans*, originally published at Oxford in 1929.

remarkable image that unites Rome with a seven-walled city: the "City Talisman" of the school of the Great Master Muhyiuddin Ibn al-`Arabi. This talisman represents the great city of the Mahdi's conquest, and therefore an eschatological Rome. Each of its circular "walls" includes a "gate," and like Tolkien's description of Minas Tirith, the gates of its walls are arranged not in a line but rather like a labyrinth. What is more, a line in this arrangement extends from its innermost circle in one direction through the other circles, very like the pier of rock towering through all the walls from the topmost level of Minas Tirith. This talisman is an esoteric representation of Rome, and not geographic; in his imaginary history, Tolkien has depicted his Rome with precisely such a geographic configuration.

The City Talisman

6

The Living Tree

Outside the Tower of Minas Tirith is the Court of the Fountain, where the "one white tree," barren and dry, was left standing through the time of the Stewards "until the King returns." Now, in Tolkien's careful structuring of the city, the ascending series of seven circular walls clearly recalls the seven levels of Heaven in traditional cosmology. The innermost or central circle of Minas Tirith therefore corresponds to the "central" or polar Heavenly sphere of the sun, and so the original designation Minas Anor or "Tower of the Sun" is perfectly appropriate. The Court of the Fountain is located in the innermost circle of the city; yet this circle is also at the summit, and so the fountain and tree particularly recall Paradise at the summit of the Heavenly spheres. In Islamic cosmology, the sacred tree of Tuba is described alongside the fountain and pool of Kawthar.

In Tolkien's cosmology, the White Tree originates from his sacred and "undying" – and so paradisical - land of Aman. There is an unmistakable medieval source for this image of the dry tree which is moreover associated with an earthly Paradise. The various designations of this motif include the Solar Tree, the Dry Tree, and the Solitary Tree, and have even been related to an Arabic source.[1] While Tolkien's tree is both solitary and dry, it is associated with the moon, and so is lunar instead of solar. Yet this medieval motif is further traced to a symbolism of two trees, of the sun and the moon, and so here Tolkien's cosmology is in agreement, since the "one white tree" is all that remains of what were formerly two trees, of the sun and the moon. In medieval legend, these trees stood on the confines of an Earthly Paradise, refusing entrance to

---

[1] J. Evola, *Le Mystère du graal et l'idée impériale gibeline*, Éditions Traditionnelles, 1967, pages 68-9. On page 61, Evola states that the Dry Tree is associated especially with a "figuration of the residence of the 'King of the World.'"

Alexander the Great while announcing his mortality.[2] As mentioned above, the example of Alexander unites sacred authority with worldly power, and so he is known as Lord of the Two Horns. In Islam there is even the possibility that he is a prophet; in the Traditions he is mentioned as one of only two believers – the other being Solomon - whose kingdom was the whole Earth. Yet despite his worldwide sovereignty, his ambition was limited by his mortality, and the domain of Paradise on Earth was not open to him. In a sense, the two trees are really two separated aspects of one symbol, belonging to a perspective outside the Earthly Paradise; the same symbol in unity, the Tree of Life, is found inside. Tolkien's dead tree corresponds to the loss of unity that is embodied in the King of the Faithful.

Another similar story is told of Alexander that relates to the fountain motif. Journeying beyond the setting sun, Alexander and his companions quest for the Fountain of Life. Once again, it is not for Alexander to attain the paradisal fountain and the undying life it bestows, yet one of his companions does. In some versions of the legend, it is his cook who discovers the fountain while preparing a fish, and the cook is very significantly named Idris. In most accounts his companion is called al-Khidr, the "Green," although the Sufi poet Nizami relates also an "account of the elders of Rome" in which his companion is Elias. So while this story also signifies the limitations of the sovereignty of Alexander, it is remarkable that another, identified with Idris and Elias and therefore the Thrice-great Hermes, has knowledge of that which Alexander hoped to attain.

Throughout its variations, the medieval motif of this tree is associated above all with an imperial sovereignty that Alexander the believer most perfectly embodied. Tolkien's tree is lunar; in the vision of Osman Ghazi, founder of the Ottoman house, the moon set into his chest, giving rise to a tree that might likewise be called lunar, and which was moreover directed towards Constantinople, or East Rome.[3] There is also a remarkable depiction of the Ottoman ruler from the Book of Sulaiman, showing this "Second Solomon" holding the "seven-ringed" and "world-revealing" ruby cup inherited from Alexander the Great,

---

[2] In an Islamic variant of this legend, the trees become one Talking Tree, but with both male and female heads, and so the symbolic duality is intact.

[3] It is believed that Shaykh Muhyiddin predicted the Ottoman state, with the tree as its emblem, in *Shajarat al-nu`maniyyah fi dawlat al-`uthmaniyyah*.

enthroned in a court amidst a fountain and tree.[4] Here the emblems of the Commander of the Faithful may be compared to the Seeing-stone and the Tree in the Court of the Fountain, both belonging rightfully to Tolkien's King of the Faithful.

In the Middle Ages, the dry tree as a motif was associated very particularly with Rome and the absence of just rule. For this reason, the "dryness" of the tree closely corresponds to the "sleep" of the Companions of the Cave, and so to the hiddenness of the saintly hierarchy in a time of injustice. In Ottoman times, the Companions of the Cave were venerated, as already mentioned, and were moreover regarded as prefiguring the seven viziers of the Mahdi. For this reason, each Ottoman vizier additionally adopted one of the names of these Companions, presumably since the names of the Mahdi's viziers were not known. The Lord of the Two Horns, whose counselors were likewise seven, and the Companions of the Cave, associated with the constellation of seven stars, are mentioned in the same chapter of the Holy Qur'an, a chapter specified in the Traditions as deserving particular attention when the time of the Antichrist approaches.[5] Furthermore, the renewal of the dry tree of Rome is associated very precisely with the eschatological victory against the armies of the Antichrist.[6] So the renewed tree, the seven stars, and the crown of the King of the Faithful,

---

[4] Reproduced in Esin Atıl, *Süleymanname: The Illustrated History of Süleyman the Magnificent*, Abrams, 1986, page 216. The caliph is here depicted as Lord of the Fortunate Conjunction, for he is enthroned on the patterns of the çintamani, a symbol related above to Tolkien's silmarilli.

[5] It should be recognized that in Tolkien's day there was an effort to improve understanding between Catholicism and Islam that emphasized the shared belief in the Companions of the Cave, most notably in the efforts of Louis Massignon; his writings on this subject mention the constellation of the Pleiades, as well as the importance of the Companions of the Cave for Rome and in eschatology. Cf. "Le culte liturgique et populaire des VII Dormants Martyrs d'Ephese (Ahl al-Kahf): Trait d'union orient-occident entre l'Islam et la Chrétienté" in *Opera Minora*, also for a calligraphic depiction of the names of the Companions in the form of a tree, quite remarkable in the present context. As regards the association of the Companions with the Pleiades, it could be said that the seven viziers in turn refer back to the constellation of the Great Bear, since it is especially these seven stars that are focused intimately on the Pole Star.

[6] Evola, *op. cit.*, page 61.

are very precise and remarkable emblems for the banner borne against the armies of the Dark Lord in *The Lord of the Rings*.

The tree, with its verticality linking the earth and sky, is a symbol of the cosmic axis or pole where Heaven and Earth meet, and especially here in conjunction with the seven stars which relate above all to the Great Bear turning around the Pole Star. The restoration of the tree in the context of eschatology signifies the uniting of Heaven and Earth in the establishment of a worldwide "Kingdom of Heaven on Earth." In the eschatology of Islam, it is for the Caliph al-Mahdi to bring healing and Heavenly rule to the Earth as the heir of the Prophet Muhammad, and further to reach that which Alexander the Great could not, since the Earthly Paradise properly belongs to the end of time. So it is appropriate that only the inheritor of the Star of Elendil is able to restore the White Tree, just as Islamic tradition holds that the presence of the Light of Muhammad could revive a dead tree. The dry and barren tree is replaced by a living tree, or rather a "tree of life." Now, the designation "white" has a particular alchemical significance, since it marks a stage in the alchemical work, as already mentioned in the individual example of Gandalf. It is reached only through "death," and is called "whitening" because it represents a purified, and so Edenic, state.

Roger Bacon was an early transmitter of the Hermetic sciences to Christendom who shared with Tolkien not only Catholicism but also a career at Oxford University. While the use of a Seeing-stone has been attributed to this "Doctor Mirabilis," the value of Alchemy was for Bacon primarily in its ability to restore the Edenic state embodied preeminently in the prophets, and so also that longevity associated with the antediluvian world. For Tolkien, the Men of the West belong properly to that antediluvian world which he calls Númenor, where the White Tree formerly grew. The longevity of the Men of the West is recalled at the precise moment of the renewal of the tree that belongs originally to the paradise of Aman, when Aragorn affirms that his longevity relates in part to his being "'of the race of the West unmingled.'" For Bacon, the science of healing belonged to the knowledge of prophets;[7] for Tolkien, the heir of the King of the Faithful has "the hands of a healer."

---

[7] Bacon's emphasis on the importance of Alchemy in medicine was later brought to its fullest development in the work of Paracelsus, whose initiation into Hermeticism is believed to have taken place in Ottoman Constantinople. This

The Hermeticism of Roger Bacon was linked to the teachings of Shihabuddin Yahya Suhrawardi, the founder of the Ishraqi "philosophy of illumination," a reformulation of Hermetic teachings which brought together the archetypes of Classical philosophy with the angelology of ancient Persia in the light of the Holy Qur'an. Already these elements have been mentioned here in relation to Tolkien's work, and indeed the legacy of Suhrawardi specifically appears in Tolkien's work in his Hidden City of Gondolin, the birthplace of Eärendil and the greatest castle of the Elves. Suhrawardi describes the hidden castle of Persia's eschatological heroes as having seven walls, each of a different material;[8] remarkably, this is also the structure of Tolkien's Gondolin. Although Gondolin belongs only to the First Age of Middle-earth, so much of its glory is reworked in the city of Gondor, with its circularity, its seven walls, its fountain, its recollection of the trees of Aman, and in the name Ecthelion that is associated with both cities. Yet while Suhrawardi's Ishraqi or Sunrise school is dedicated to the light of the East, there is no doubt that Tolkien is turned to the light of the West.

Roger Bacon's study of Alchemy has specifically been traced to his discovery of an Arabic book which purports to contain the esoteric teachings of Aristotle to Alexander the Great, including teachings on physiognomic discernment. He makes extensive reference to this book in his writings, and produced a commentary entitled *Secretum Secretorum*[9] that significantly also includes the Emerald Tablet of Hermes Trismegistos, an ancient text that is considered the essence of Latin Alchemy and has its earliest formulation in the Alchemy of Islam. According to Islamic sources, the Emerald Tablet was received by

---

branch of Hermeticism was still later represented at Oxford in the work of Robert Fludd.

[8] Cf. Henry Corbin, *Face de Dieu, Face de l'homme*.

[9] Some attention is given to alchemical elixirs in the *Secretum Secretorum*. For his part, Tolkien alludes to the elixirs of Alchemy throughout *The Lord of the Rings*, from the miruvor of the Elves to the Ent-draughts to the use of kingsfoil in the Houses of Healing. Still, such elixirs have their proper use, and are no remedy for death. Tolkien illustrates the Númenórean error of seeking "endless life unchanging" with the precise imagery of a degenerate Hermeticism: "'Childless lords sat in aged halls musing on heraldry; in secret chambers withered men compounded strong elixirs, or in high cold towers asked questions of the stars'" ("The Window on the West"). The last example, of course, is in exact contrast to the already mentioned description of "wise men that watched the stars."

Apollonius of Tyana, the "Master of Talismans,"[10] directly from Hermes in an underground chamber, and in turn passed it on to Aristotle who delivered it to Alexander the Great.

ROGER BACON an Inglishman.

      Roger Bacon's Arabic source was *Sirr al-Asrar*, that around the same time provided the model for a study by the Great Master Muhyiuddin Ibn al-`Arabi on the correspondences between the macrocosm of a kingdom and the microcosm. The Great Master later produced a very remarkable sequel that bears a very remarkable title: *The Fabulous Roc in the Knowledge of the Western Sun and the Seal of the Saints.*[11] This work is devoted to the light of the West, or rather to the reality of the Western Sun in the Caliph al-Mahdi. This work is the source of the City Talisman that was compared to the structure of Minas Tirith. So here, from an Arabic source containing the knowledges

---

[10] Indeed the Alchemist Jabir Ibn Hayyan cites Apollonius as his source for the talismanic square of "three times three."

[11] Cf. Gerald Elmore, *Islamic Sainthood in the Fullness of Time*, Brill, 1999. This study includes a list of the extant manuscripts of the *Fabulous Roc*, and one of these is in the possession of the Vatican in Rome.

appropriate to Alexander the Great, the heritage of Bacon's alchemy contained in the work of another Catholic at Oxford unexpectedly reunites after seven centuries with a greater development of the *Sirr al-Asrar* that belongs to the mysticism of Islam. This alchemical legacy has been renewed like the tree from the legend of Alexander, in the light of the Western Sun that rises from an eschatological Paradise.

7

Stone of the Saint

Concerning the title, *The Fabulous Roc in the Knowledge of the Western Sun and the Seal of the Saints*, the translation of "roc"[1] for the Arabic "`anqa'" may not be exact; in fact a much better image of the mysterious `anqa' than the Eagles of *The Lord of the Rings* could hardly be imagined. The dominant characteristic of this bird of Arab mythology is that of an eagle of tremendous size and altogether supernatural aspect. Tolkien's choice of "Eagle" moreover establishes an association at once with the emblem of Imperial Rome[2] and with the Black Banner of the Holy Prophet named the Eagle; yet even more precisely, in the writings of Paracelsus the alchemical phoenix is called the "Flying Eagle". When Gandalf through "fire and death" is transformed into Gandalf the White, it is the Lord of the Eagles who appears to signal the phoenix-like rebirth of the Wizard saint. When Aragorn enters the city of Minas Tirith after passing through the "Paths of the Dead" and the fires of war, he is recognized by the green stone set in his Eagle ornament as the prophesied King Elessar, meaning "Elfstone." What is more, when Aragorn had visited the city of Minas Tirith in his youth, he did so as Thorongil, "Eagle of the Star."

The association of Tolkien's Eagle with the green gem or emerald recalls the emerald mountain of Qaf, believed to be the home of the roc. This emerald mountain of Islamic cosmology encircles the world and is located at its extreme limit;[3] it is therefore the meeting place of

---

[1] The Rook or Castle of the game of Chess adapted by Christendom from the world of Islam combines the meanings of roc, tower, and champion of chivalry.

[2] The `anqa' is moreover an emblem of the Ottoman dynasty.

[3] So it is significant that Tolkien traces his Eagles to the inaccessible "Encircling Mountains." This was moreover the location of the Hidden City of Gondolin, the Persian prototype of which is also linked to the sacred geography of Qaf.

Heaven and Earth. Both the emerald of this mountain and the giant roc that rules between earth and sky symbolize in Islam the saint who in this earthly life attains to his Heavenly authority. So the Eagle, or rather the "Fabulous Roc" of Middle-earth, holds the Elfstone that is the sign of King Elessar, the "Western Sun;" and it is not too difficult to perceive in Gandalf, the wisest saint in Middle-earth and the arranger of the good at the end of an age, and who is repeatedly borne by the Lord of the Eagles, a suggestion of the station of the "Seal of the Saints,"[4] at least for the Third Age: "'for he has been the mover of all that has been accomplished, and this is his victory.'"[5]

The green gem of the Elfstone is itself mentioned early in the events of *The Lord of the Rings*; it is made a distinguishing mark of Eärendil by design, and the teller of the story of Eärendil is afterwards made to say of his work, "'As a matter of fact it was all mine. Except that Aragorn insisted on my putting in a green stone. He seemed to think it important. I don't know why. Otherwise he obviously thought the whole thing rather above my head...'"[6] Such is the case with Tolkien's tale, in which the presence of the Elfstone is essential, even if many "don't know why."

Because of the sanctity and wisdom of Tolkien's Elves, the Elfstone is properly a "Saint-stone" or "Stone of the Wise." Now "Stone of the Wise," or rather "Philosopher's Stone," belongs to the language of Alchemy, and designates the mystery that is revealed in the Great Work. This association is supported by the manner in which the Elfstone appears in the story, first when Aragorn receives it after the passage of the tomb of Moria, and second when by means of it he is recognized as the prophesied king in Minas Tirith, following his braving of the Paths of the Dead. In either case, the Elfstone appears following a purifying descent into the Earth, and so each process suggests the renowned alchemical teaching attributed to Basilius Valentinus: "Visit the interior of the Earth; through purification thou wilt find the hidden stone." The green gem moreover recalls the Emerald Tablet of Hermes Trismegistos,

---

[4] In the *Fabulous Roc* this "Seal of the Saints" is associated with the ruby, and so it is significant that Gandalf wears the ruby Elven ring.

[5] "The Steward and the King." This may be compared to the honoring of the Sufi master Ak Shamsuddin by Mehmed the Conqueror in the Ottoman victory at Constantinople; what is more, "ak" means "white" and "shams" means "sun."

[6] "Many Meetings," *The Fellowship of the Ring*.

and since this tablet reveals the essence of Alchemy, it is not surprising that the emerald itself has been identified with the Philosopher's Stone. Possession of the Stone was especially associated with longevity, indeed "Arabian alchemists were the first to ascribe therapeutic properties to the Stone, and it was through Arabian alchemy that the conception of the *Elixir Vitae* came to the West."[7] Elessar the Elfstone affirms that "'being what I am...I shall have life far longer than other men.'"[8]

An essential teaching of the Emerald Tablet is that the "little world" of the individual shares a pattern with the outer "larger world." Such a relationship is also expressed in the language of the Holy Qur'an: "We shall show them Our signs on the horizons and within themselves until it will be manifest unto them that it is the Truth."[9] In the *Fabulous Roc*, this teaching is brought to fulfillment, with eschatology presented as but a manifestation in the outer world of the inner reality of the completion of the saint. This inward aspect of eschatology likewise has a part in *The Lord of the Rings*, concerning the path that Frodo the Ring-bearer must follow to undo the evil of the Enemy. The Ring-bearer experiences a series of "deaths" and "resurrections" along that path, and so Frodo's quest embodies the inward journey of the soul that is initiated into the mysteries. The series of "deaths" brings the subtleties of the Hermetic work into focus; here it should simply be observed that in the initiatic journey "every change of state whatsoever is at once a death and a birth," and that "the changes undergone by the being in the course of its development are really indefinite in number."[10] No doubt Tolkien has made the significance of these initiatic deaths all the more clear when, as at the Ford of Rivendell or the entry into Mordor, Frodo is "resurrected" at an explicitly new stage of his journey. Ultimately the Lord of the Eagles appears not only for Gandalf; he appears also to raise Frodo and his servant Sam from the fires of Mount Doom, when at last they are purified of the One Ring and the personification of its effects on the "little world," Gollum. In Islamic mysticism, three terms identify aspects

---

[7] Mircea Eliade, *The Forge and the Crucible*, University of Chicago, 1978, page 167.

[8] "The Steward and the King." This, then, is a reality parodied by the unnatural preservation offered by the One Ring. Similarly, the Ringwraiths' "Black Breath" may be identified as an inversion of the breath of the King that accompanies the use of kingsfoil in the Houses of Healing.

[9] XLI, 53.

[10] Guénon, *Perspectives on Initiation*, pages 172-3.

of the soul: nafs al-ammarah bil-su' (the soul which incites to evil), nafs al-lawwamah (the reproving soul), and nafs al-mutma'inah (the soul at peace). These three aspects of the soul are well embodied in Gollum, Sam, and Frodo, respectively, and it should not be overlooked that this is likewise a significance of the St. George and the Dragon iconography.[11] The attainment of sainthood is signaled by the descent of the Sakinah in the heart and the attainment of the soul at peace.

For the macrocosm of the seven-walled city, an Eagle descends to herald the attainment of the Ring-bearer. At the moment that his quest is fulfilled, "the Shadow departed, and the Sun was unveiled, and light leaped forth; and the waters of Anduin shone like silver, and in all the houses of the City men sang for the joy that welled up in their hearts from what source they could not tell."[12] Both inward and outward aspects of eschatology in *The Lord of the Rings*, having separated into two distinct storylines by the close of the first volume, are reunited in the third, at the Field of Cormallen. Not only does this location evoke the gardens of Paradise, but its name moreover means "circle of gold," only this gold is a gold which may not be hoarded. Indeed Cormallen signals the alchemical transmutation that is attained through the unmaking of that which was its counterfeit, the circle of gold of the One Ring. This process is known as "solve et coagula," to "dissolve and coagulate" in a more perfect form.[13]

Gold is among metals as the sun is among the heavenly bodies, and a circle with a point at its center symbolizes both gold and the sun. In a posthumously published essay on the Elfstone, Tolkien describes the jewel as holding the light of the Sun.[14] The Philosopher's Stone is also called the "Solar Stone," since the last stage of the alchemical work is reached at a level which corresponds to that of the sun in the Heavenly order. Having passed through the stages of the alchemical work,

---

[11] In this example the horse represents the middle aspect. Indeed it should be noted that Tolkien suggests in subtle ways this particular iconography, especially in the Hobbits' first struggle with Gollum. St. George, of course, is the patron saint of England and the Order of the Garter, and is known in Islam as al-Khidr, the Green Man.

[12] "The Steward and the King."

[13] This process is prefigured on a smaller scale when Gandalf "dissolves" the influence of Wormtongue and so becomes the counselor of the renewed "King of the Golden Hall."

[14] "The Elessar," *Unfinished Tales*.

identified above as first lunar and then solar, Aragorn reaches the Tower of the Western Sun, and so in this sense the King Elessar, already identified with the Western Sun of Islamic eschatology, is the "completion" of the events of the Third Age of Middle-earth.[15] In Tolkien's words, the city had "passed through darkness and fire to a new day," when "the King would enter his gates with the rising of the Sun."[16]

The colors of the alchemical stages are recalled when, from a casket of "black," the "White" Crown is revealed, bearing a jewel "the light of which went up like a flame."[17] What is more, the wings of the Crown recall the winged cap of Hermes, and also the wings atop the staff of the caduceus, especially since the Númenórean heirlooms brought from Rivendell refer to this key of the alchemical work: the Sceptre of Annúminas provides the axis of the "Staff of Hermes," and so depicts the cosmic axis or pole;[18] the "twin serpents" of the Ring of Barahir complete the iconography. The Ring of Barahir anciently represents in Tolkien's imagination the uniting of the Two Kindreds of Men and Elves, and of course the Two Kindreds are reunited with the long-awaited marriage of the king with Arwen Evenstar. And while it may be said that the completion of Alchemy is best symbolized by the "marriage" by which the sun and moon are conjoined, Tolkien has the solar Elessar married with a light of the evening that is not specifically lunar; yet it is the very designation "Evenstar" that suggests a

---

[15] This alchemical completion corresponds to the placing of the cornerstone in architectural symbolism, as René Guénon has observed in his article on the subject ("The Cornerstone," *Fundamental Symbols of Sacred Science*). It is significant that, just as Guénon has associated the cornerstone at the same time with Alchemy and the literal meaning of "chief," Tolkien's Elfstone is also the "Chieftain" of the Dúnedain. And it must further be recognized that inasmuch as the cornerstone represents both principle and final achievement, its symbolism has a particularly Muhammadan significance, since the Light of Muhammad is considered the principle of creation, embodied in the last and Seal of the Prophets. In the words of the Prophet Muhammad: "My place among the prophets is as when a man builds a wall and completes it except for one brick. I am that brick, and after me there is neither messenger nor prophet."

[16] "The Steward and the King."

[17] *Ibid.*

[18] For this reason the sceptre had not previously been delivered to Aragorn, as Elrond had told him: "The Sceptre of Annúminas I withhold, for you have yet to earn it" (appendix A).

transcendent aspect not unrelated to the Star of Elendil, and so this marriage manifests at once the completion of the king's attainment as well as a renewed sanctification of the rule of Men by the heiress of a timeless sanctity.

Now the success of alchemical transmutation depends upon the presence of the Philosopher's Stone. By means of this stone, gold is produced in the domain of minerals; the regeneration of a tree is accomplished in the vegetable domain; and among animals, the Phoenix is reborn from the ashes. Tolkien does not fail to include each in his alchemical description of Aragorn who is the Elfstone and the Eagle of the Star: "All that is gold does not glitter...Deep roots are not reached by the frost...From the ashes a fire shall be woken."[19] According to the Rosicrucian tradition of Hermeticism, that originally received its inspiration very directly from Islamic sources,[20] the Great Work of Alchemy is presided over by Elias Artista, who dwells in the "Solar Citadel" "which is moreover the abode of the 'Immortals' and which represents one of the aspects of the 'Center of the World.'" [21] Here the identification of Tolkien's Tower of the Sun with the Solar Citadel is obvious enough. It should also not be surprising that the forms of the Thrice-Great Hermes should converge at the unity of the "center;" for Tolkien has not merely included the symbols of Hermes[22] in the ascension of his long-lived king. Just as Eärendil, the original bearer of the Elfstone, has been related to the prophets Idris and Elias, so Elessar in his solar tower recalls not only Idris in his solar residence, but even more so Elias Artista, the specifically alchemical formulation of the

---

[19] Since Tolkien singled out the importance of the element ar- in Aragorn's name, it is interesting to recall that according to Sebottendorf, the rune ar "signifies Aryan, primal fire, the sun, and the eagle" (quoted in Joscelyn Godwin, *Arktos*, Adventures Unlimited, 1996, page 55).

[20] Cf. especially "Rose-Cross & Rosicrucians" in Guénon's *Perspectives on Initiation*. In this connection, it is interesting to note that the emblem of the "mystic rose" adorning the taj or "crown" of the followers of the Sufi master `Abdul-Qadir Jilani contained precisely those colors related to the alchemical work, and that at the center of this rose was depicted the Seal of Solomon, although by the nineteenth century the pentagram was depicted more explicitly.

[21] René Guénon, "Hermes," *The Sword of Gnosis*, Penguin, 1974, page 375.

[22] Since "winged sandals" belong to Hermes, the name "Wingfoot" for Aragorn should be recalled as yet another example.

Eliatic function.[23] For Paracelsus, this Elias Artista had yet to appear, and he moreover foretold that at the time of his coming "there shall be nothing so hidden that it shall not be revealed." Not only do these words recall the alchemical formulation of the "hidden stone," but most remarkably the name Elessar itself – the name "foretold" for the owner of the Elfstone – evokes the alchemists' expectation of Elias Artista, since both names share the letters El-s-ar.

In his central and solar position, the King is "revealed' in a luminous form that unites heavenly authority and earthly power: "wisdom sat upon his brow, and strength and healing were in his hands, and a light was about him."[24] Since the Seal of Solomon served in the language of Alchemy very precisely as a symbol of the Philosopher's Stone, the six-pointed star of the Star of Elendil diadem is a sign of the reality shared by Elendil and his heir, a reality that is both the goal of Alchemy as well as that which may accomplish the alchemical transmutation, and so may be said to transcend both lunar and solar. Here the two triangles of the star represent the spirit and body of the saint, in whom "the spirit has become materialized and the material body spiritualized." Now the Star of Elendil belongs to the heritage of Arnor, and so is called "Star of the North," a designation that at the same time emphasizes the polar function of its bearer. As far as the emblems of Gondor borne on the banner of the King are concerned, it is not a star that signifies this unique function, since there are seven stars, but rather the winged crown surmounting the axial Tree. The King's reuniting of the diadem and the crown represents a conjunction of worldly realms, and so may be said to take place at the center of a worldly and therefore "horizontal" dimension. Yet the two triangles of the Seal of Solomon above all symbolize the conjunction of Heaven and Earth that belongs to a dimension "vertical" in relation to the world. And since it is even more explicitly the Tree of Gondor that embodies such a vertical axis, the wings of the crown surmounting the Tree moreover signify the ascent of the King's glory. This vertical movement has been prefigured in his name, "Eagle of the Star," and is signaled by the jewel at the summit of his crown, "the light of which went up like a flame." According to the

---

[23] That so many formulations of Elias are not out of keeping with the reality of his function is suggested by the salutation on the prophet in the Holy Qur'an (XXXVII, 130), in which the name Elias actually appears in the plural form.
[24] "The Steward and the King."

Emerald Tablet: "It rises from Earth to Heaven and comes down again from Heaven to Earth, and thus acquires the power of the realities above and the realities below. In this way you will acquire the glory of the whole world, and all darkness will leave you."

The attainment of the center in the worldly dimension is properly the realization of the lesser mysteries, and this in turn opens onto the realization of higher states, at least virtually, because these states may only be reached from the center by way of the axis. The solar manifestation at the center of the world corresponds to the center of the heavenly realm only because of the presence of this axis or Pole, and so it is by this axis that the solar embodiment in the world shares in the realities of Idris and Mitatrun, the heavenly representatives of the Light of Muhammad.[25] This axis is properly the domain of the greater mysteries realized by the Perfect Man (al-insan al-kamil).[26] Remarkably, two emblems of verticality in the traditions of Tolkien's Men are the Pillar of Heaven of Númenor and the White Tree, and both "Pillar of Heaven" and "Tree" are symbolic designations of the Perfect Man in the writings of Shaykh Muhyiuddin Ibn al-`Arabi.

While it is the King who wields the Sword Reforged and "whose hands bring healing," it should not be overlooked that "a deadly sword, a healing hand" likewise identifies Gandalf-Mithrandir;[27] and whereas Mithrandir had been told, "'the Sun shines through you,'" this phrase applies likewise to Elessar in his solar attainment at the center of Middle-earth. With the attainment of Elessar, Gandalf – whose polar function is affirmed in the description, "the mover of all that has been accomplished" – announces to the King his departure from Middle-earth, as they stand upon the hallow of Mount Mindolluin:

> "This is your realm, and the heart of the greater realm that shall be. The Third Age of the world is ended, and the new age is begun; and it is your task to order its beginning and to preserve what may be preserved…The Third Age was my age.

---

[25] Polar symbolism may therefore be said to have precedence over the solar.

[26] Cf. on these matters René Guénon, *Symbolism of the Cross*. The progression of realization from the horizontal to the vertical is best exemplified by the Night Journey and Ascension of the Prophet Muhammad.

[27] "The Mirror of Galadriel," *The Fellowship of the Ring*.

> I was the enemy of Sauron; and my work is finished. I shall go
> soon. The burden must lie now upon you and your kindred."[28]

These words refer to a responsibility that had belonged to Gandalf – and
no doubt had in some measure belonged to Eärendil and Elendil in
former Ages – that in turn is inherited by Elessar at the "heart" or center
of the "greater realm" or macrocosm.[29] This role is at were confirmed by
the discovery at the hallow of the White Tree, that is a living
embodiment of a connection both to the paradise of Aman as well as to
the temporal origin of things. For the Third Age, the very same may be
said of the "angelic" origin of Mithrandir; and just as the White Tree was
borne on the banner of Elendil and his heir, so did Aragorn say of
Gandalf's unique function: "'you are our captain and our banner. The
Dark Lord has Nine, but we have One, mightier than they: the White
Rider.'"[30]

This saintly function inherited by King Elfstone is both at the
center and at the summit of a world, a function that - hidden or manifest
- must be preserved, since "without a center nothing could actually
exist."[31] In the words of Shaykh Muhyiuddin Ibn al-`Arabi:

> The world subsists in virtue of his existence. He is to the world
> what the setting of a seal is to the seal: that is to say the place
> where the imprint is engraved, the symbol with which the king
> seals his treasures. This is why he has been called caliph: for
> through him God preserves His creation, as the seal preserves
> the treasures. As long as the king's seal remains unbroken, no
> one would dare to open the treasures without his permission.
> Thus Man has been charged to guard the kingdom, and the
> world will be preserved for as long as the Perfect Man subsists
> therein.[32]

---

[28] "The Steward and the King."

[29] This chain of succession is prefigured in *The Fellowship of the Ring* ("Farewell to
Lórien") when it is said of Aragorn that "in Moria the burden of Gandalf had
been laid on him," temporarily at first, during the "death" of the latter. It may
even be observed that the polar function of Aragorn is foreshadowed by
Tolkien's only explicit reference to the polar constellation of the Great Bear, on
the first night of Aragorn's appearance in the story ("Strider").

[30] "The White Rider."

[31] René Guénon, *The Great Triad.*

[32] Quoted in Chodkiewicz, *op. cit.*, page 70.

So the King recalls the words of Elendil when he is crowned: "Out of the Great Sea to Middle-earth I am come. In this place will I abide, and my heirs, unto the ending of the world."[33]

---

[33] "The Steward and the King."

8

The Grail Family

There is yet another mystery of the Middle Ages associated with the green stone, a mystery that persists and is called the Grail. One account of its origin identifies the Grail as an emerald that separated from the forehead or "crown" of Lucifer at his fall; in *The Silmarillion*, Tolkien recounts how the silmaril of Eärendil had been retrieved from the crown of Morgoth, formerly Melkor, the master of Sauron.[1] No less significant is Tolkien's description of the Elfstone: "For it is said that those who looked through this stone saw things that were withered or burned healed again or as they were in the grace of their youth, and that the hands of one who held it brought to all that they touched healing from hurt."[2] This may be compared to the description of the Grail, a description that, it should be observed, refers first and foremost to the "Flying Eagle" of Alchemy:

> By the power of that stone the phoenix burns to ashes, but the ashes give him life again...There never was a human so ill but that, if he one day sees that stone, he cannot die within the week that follows...His appearance will stay the same, be it maid or man, as on the day he saw the stone, the same as when the best years of his life began...Such power does the stone give a man that flesh and bones are at once made young again.[3]

---

[1] Again, in Islam it is Satan's envy for the Light of Muhammad on the brow of man that is the cause of his fall. Morgoth's crown is but a mockery of the heavenly attainment that Eärendil achieves with the silmaril on his brow.

[2] "The Elessar."

[3] Wolfram von Eschenbach, *Parzival*, translated by Mustard and Passage, Vintage, 1961, page 251-2.

There have been two branches in the development of the Grail legend from a pagan foundation which is obscure, even with the acknowledgement of the Mithraic influence: one that may be identified as Hermetic, in which the Grail is a stone, and the other Ecclesiastic, in which a mystery from beyond Christendom was brought into conformity with the doctrine of the Crucifixion, and so became a chalice in conformity with Church ritual. Not surprisingly, the Hermetic branch of the legend very clearly expresses its connection to Islam, most especially in the *Parzival* of Wolfram von Eschenbach, the first complete version of the legend that is also the source of the above description of the Grail.

Not only does *Parzival* trace its source to Muslim Spain, but the attainment of the Grail even follows Parzival's reconciliation with his Muslim brother Feirefiz, who has a strange piebald appearance.[4] What is more, the attainment of the Grail brings the healing of the keeper of the Grail and his realm, with the asking of a question concerning the king's ailment; in fact, the king had been wounded in a joust, fighting with impurity against a Muslim knight from the borders of Paradise who fought with the name of the Grail. The Earthly Paradise, as mentioned previously, signifies the meeting place of Heaven and Earth; the black and white skin of Feirefiz likewise refers to the union of a cosmic duality.[5] So the reconciliation of Parzival brings with it the redemption of the king's transgression, and both are in relation to that knighthood that unifies Heaven and Earth.

Already the correspondence between chivalry and Hermeticism has been alluded to, but here in the Grail legend these two forms of "royal art" converge. The authors of *The Krater and the Grail* have identified an important source for Wolfram's *Parzival* in the "Corpus Hermeticum" preserved by Islam; yet no less important was the influence of spiritual chivalry (futuwwah), literally the "way of youth."[6]

---

[4] Cf. Pierre Ponsoye, *L'Islam et le Graal: Étude sur l'ésotérisme du Parzival de Wolfram von Eschenbach*, Arché, 1976.

[5] The best-known symbol of this is the yin-yang of China, although the piebald banner of the Knights Templar is perhaps a better example here. It should be noted that the guards in Minas Tirith are garbed in black and white, the "livery of the heirs of Elendil" ("Minas Tirith," *The Return of the King*); for his part, King Elessar appears in black armor with a white mantle.

[6] Cf. the introduction to *The Royal Book of Spiritual Chivalry*. It should be mentioned that an initiatory ritual of futuwwah was the drinking of salt

Wolfram von Eschenbach was himself a knight, and in his day there was a great revival of spiritual chivalry under the authority of the caliphate, that the author of *Parzival* calls "the supreme power on earth over all lands." Centered in the Round City of Baghdad, this revival was under the direction of the caliph's advisor, the Sufi master Shihabuddin `Umar Suhrawardi, who described in his Book of Futuwwah how spiritual chivalry originated. According to Suhrawardi, all the prophets possessed spiritual chivalry, yet in the time of the prophet Abraham, an "island" of futuwwah was given to his chivalrous companions who were not able to "sail" on the "sea" of Sufism all the way to its end. This description provides another model for understanding the distinction between the greater mysteries of Sufism and the lesser mysteries of chivalry and Hermeticism alike, since the island abode corresponds to the lesser mysteries, whereas Sufism leads ultimately to the greater mysteries of the Divine Realm. It must also be observed how closely this description accords with Tolkien's island of Númenor, for it too was a divine gift, and especially for Men whose chivalry aided the Elves in the First Age of Middle-earth yet who were not able to sail all the way to the shores of Aman.[7] In the Holy Qur'an, the exemplars of spiritual chivalry are the

---

dissolved in water, the preparation of which corresponds to the "solve" of Alchemy.

[7] Again, Eärendil had reached Aman and so may be understood to have attained the greater mysteries, as his emblem signifies; Tolkien also suggests as much for the father of Elendil. As far as these greater mysteries of Aman are concerned, they could still be attained in the Third Age by sailing along what Tolkien calls the "Straight Way," a variation of the vertical axis that warrants comparison with the "Straight Path" (sirat al-mustaqim) mentioned in the first chapter of the Holy Qur'an (cf. Guénon, *Symbolism of the Cross*). This Straight Way is open only to the saintly Elves, as well as to those who attain sanctity, like the trustworthy Ring-bearers and Gimli the Dwarf, whose attainment proceeds from his pure devotion to the Elven Lady Galadriel. The verticality of this Straight Way for the Elves and their friends is suggested by the traditional form of Elven ships, for they were made in the likeness of swans, and birds and their wings signify ascent above all, as already mentioned in connection with the winged crown. This verticality is also recognizable by its inverse, most explicitly in the descent of the armada of Ar-Pharazôn into an "abyss" for sailing against Aman. Indeed the parody of the polar function – like Hitler and his swastika – brings the inversion of ascension or rather the descent into lower states. The Straight Path of the Holy Qur'an is described as "the path of those on whom is Thy grace," and since grace descends from above, this relates to the descent of the Sakinah upon the heart; it is

Companions of the Cave, whose youth was miraculously preserved through hundreds of years. Here the conjunction of youth and supernatural longevity recalls especially the motif of the Fountain of Life from the legend of Alexander the Great.[8] Tolkien for his part specifically mentions the fountains brought from the Blessed Realm to Númenor, as well as the supernatural longevity granted to the Númenóreans.[9] The remarkable accord of Tolkien's vision with Suhrawardi's teaching ends with the fall of Númenor; still, the chivalry of the Faithful is preserved in Minas Tirith, that Tolkien calls the "last memory" of Númenor.[10]

In his treatment of the Elfstone, Tolkien reformulates the "Hermetic" Grail, and, perhaps remarkably, not that of his own Catholicism. Indeed, unlike the upholding of chastity in the Ecclesiastic branch of the legend, the Hermetic branch includes the symbolism of marriage, as does *The Lord of the Rings*. More exactly, the marriage of the maiden who bears the Grail at the conclusion of *Parzival* corresponds to the marriage of Arwen Evenstar, especially since the Elfstone had formerly been in her keeping. Furthermore, the marriage of the Grail maiden is linked to a baptismal font of ruby, the redness of which relates to the attainment of the alchemical marriage. Now, immediately after the wedding of Elessar and Arwen, they appear at the fountain by the Tree. This image recalls the motif of medieval art called the "Tryst Beneath the Tree," which like the Grail is from Arthurian legend. A most remarkable example of this motif is found decorating the ceiling in the Hall of Justice

---

therefore not the path "of those on whom is Thy anger," who thus fall away from the transcendent into lower states, "nor of those who go astray," who sail, as it were, separated from the axis on roads which Tolkien calls "bent."

[8] Remarkably, the Fountain of Life was located in the far West. Already this motif has been associated with al-Khidr, "the only Moslem saint who goes on horseback" (Hasluck, *op.cit.*, page 327 note 5) who is moreover identified with the chivalric St. George, and with Idris and Elias, two forms of the Thrice-great Hermes. The perennity of al-Khidr's Sufi chivalry corresponds to the perennity of Hermes' sciences, and so in both cases "lesser mysteries" are preserved by figures possessed of supernatural longevity. In fact, these three figures – al-Khidr, Idris, and Elias – belong to an exalted rank in the spiritual hierarchy of Islamic mysticism according to Ibn al-`Arabi, that of the four Awtad or Pillars

[9] "Akallabêth," *The Silmarillion*.

[10] "The Field of Cormallen," *The Return of the King*.

in the Alhambra or "Red Fortress" of Granada,[11] a city associated above with the "Prophecy of the Red Apple," and so with Minas Tirith.[12] The paintings on this ceiling of the Alhambra are unique indeed, for they represent a Muslim expression of Arthurian motifs, some even taken from the Grail quest, in the land that was the source of Wolfram's account of the Grail, albeit before these particular motifs were painted.[13] Here the "Tryst Beneath the Tree" depicts a man and woman flanking a fountain adorned with lions, and the fountain moreover contains youthful figures, so that it is at the same time a "Fountain of Life."

The alchemical marriage of sulphur and quicksilver is here symbolized not only by the man and woman, but also by the lions and waters, since the lion is a solar symbol like the red ruby, complementing the lunar element of water.[14] The paintings of the Alhambra ceiling are moreover aligned in relation to a centerpiece of this last stronghold of Islam in Spain, the Court of Lions, where a ring of twelve stone lions of unknown origin supports its fountain. Twelve, of course, is a solar number, since the sun's yearly cycle is divided principally into twelve. This lion fountain of the Alhambra has long been associated with the prophet-king Solomon,[15] whose legacy is moreover omnipresent in the legends of the Grail. More remarkably, the structure surrounding the Court of the Lions has been shown to evoke a certain royal temple of ancient Persia, now called the Throne of Solomon, that is the very temple

---

[11] Cf. Jerrilynn D. Dodds in "The Paintings in the Sala de Justicia of the Alhambra: Iconography and Iconology," *The Art Bulletin*, volume 61/2.

[12] Perhaps the best-known example of the talismanic use of the hand is carved in stone above the gate of the Alhambra in the keystone of its arch. Since Gandalf has already been associated with the talismanic hand, it is interesting that it is Gandalf, with his horse "steadfast as a graven image," that alone guards the gate of Minas Tirith in "The Siege of Gondor" (*The Return of the King*).

[13] These paintings deserve further study. As far as *The Lord of the Rings* is concerned, they also include a depiction of the medieval Wild Man or Wodewose who is equivalent to Tolkien's Woses.

[14] It should be observed that Tolkien's fountain in Minas Tirith is also a "lion fountain," insofar as it is associated with the name Ecthelion, for not only was the fate of this Elf warrior bound up with the "lion-headed" Lord of Balrogs, but Tolkien even identifies him as Ecthelion of the Fountain, a title that combines "fountain" with the word "lion" that forms the ending of his name.

[15] Cf. Oleg Grabar, *The Alhambra*, Harvard University, 1978, pages 127-9.

proven to be the model for the legendary Grail Castle.[16] Since this legendary castle is more generally placed atop a mountain, enclosed by a wall, and alongside a body of water, the geography of Minas Tirith is comparable to that of the Grail Castle.[17]

In *Parzival*, the waters of the baptismal font flow from the power of the Grail. The authors of *The Krater and the Grail* have identified the apparently Christian motif of baptism rather as an adaptation of a Hermetic teaching. Symbolic baptism in the Hermetic Krater brought gnosis, and so in *Parzival* baptism brings a form of gnosis expressed by the ability to see the Grail; and again, it is the vision of the Grail that bestows youth like the legendary Fountain of Life. In Arabic, the word `ayn signifies both fountain and eye, and among the names of the Prophet of Islam is `Ayn al-Ghurr, the Fountain of the Luminous Marks of Nobleness. These "luminous marks" are remarkably linked to the ritual ablution – and so the daily "baptism" - of the Muslim. According to Tradition, the Prophet Muhammad distinguished his Companions from his "brothers" who had yet to appear, identifying the latter by the luminous marks on their foreheads; these marks – the ghurr - appear as a consequence of his brothers' ritual ablutions, and the Prophet promises to lead these brothers to the paradise pool of Kawthar. Once again the motif of the luminous forehead appears, and like the light of faith, the "luminous marks of nobleness" manifest in that place associated with the Light of Muhammad;[18] and it should be noted that those so marked are identified as the Prophet's "brothers," and therefore belonging to his "family." In the traditions of spiritual chivalry, the "way of youth" has its source in the Light of Muhammad, and in traditional histories this

---

[16] Cf. Grabar, *op. cit.*, page 148; and Arthur Upham Pope, "Persia and the Holy Grail," *The Literary Review*, I, 1957.

[17] In 1926, Lewis Spence had described a circular Grail Castle as an "indubitable memory" of Atlantis (*The History of Atlantis*, Bell, page 133); this claim is remarkably analogous to Tolkien's description of Minas Tirith as "the last memory" of Númenor-Atlantis. Indeed it is especially in their circularity that these castles recall the form of the Atlantean city. The original plan of Baghdad should also be noted.

[18] Now the significance of the eye, worn as a red mark on the helmeted foreheads of the servants of the Dark Lord, appears as the sinister parody of that luminous sign the source of which is at once both Fountain and Eye. Since the Eye of Sauron appears on helmets, this may specifically be contrasted with another Tradition, "The armament of the faithful is ablution."

light is compared to a white gem endowed with all the properties of the waters of Paradise.[19]

> The inner eye is enlightened by spiritual chivalry,
> The garden of the soul blooms from spiritual chivalry,
> If there is knowledge of spiritual chivalry in your head,
> It will continue to bestow felicity upon felicity upon you.[20]

At the fountain in Minas Tirith, "while the Tree grew and blossomed," Frodo receives not only a "white gem like a star," but moreover the promise of the Elven paradise.[21]

Whereas the Prophet Muhammad was the Seal of Prophecy, his descendant al-Mahdi is the expected Seal of Spiritual Chivalry; `Ali, about whom it is said, "There is no chivalrous youth if not `Ali, there is no sword if not Dhul-Fiqar," is considered the historical Pole of Spiritual Chivalry. The Family of the Prophet is traced to the marriage of his daughter Fatima with `Ali, who is moreover known by the title "Victorious Lion of God." Their son Husayn, the third Imam of this Noble Family, is reported to have related this alchemical formula: "`Ali was the gold, Fatima was the silver, I am the son of the gold and the silver. My father was the sun, my mother was the moon, I am the son of

---

[19] Hajjah Amina Adil, *op. cit.* Nizami calls the Fountain of Life a "fountain of light."

[20] Quoted in *The Royal Book of Spiritual Chivalry*, page 3.

[21] "Many Partings." The conjunction of the waters of a fountain with a star recalls the Phial of Galadriel, in which light from the Star of Eärendil was set amid the waters of Galadriel's fountain. Both white gem and phial embody a most profound conjunction of the transcendent with the purest material. The white gem is worn particularly "in memory of Elfstone and Evenstar;" even so, it might seem that the attainment of Elessar and Arwen is incomplete because their fate is to pass away in Middle-earth, and not to sail to Aman. Their fate is therefore not unlike that of Elendil the Elf-friend, and yet distinct from the fate of those preserved in the Blessed Realm. However, such a distinction among saints is mentioned in the Holy Qur'an: "Of the believers are men who are true to that which they covenanted with Allah. Some of them have paid their vow by death, and some of them still are waiting..." (XXXIII, 23). And while these saints are called "men," according to Muhyiuddin Ibn al-`Arabi, "there is no spiritual quality belonging to men to which women do not have equal access" (Quoted in Chodkiewicz, *op. cit.*, page 98). In all cases, of course, Tolkien presents sanctity, and sanctification, in Elven terms.

the sun and the moon."[22] The Imams are twelve in succession, even though many generations have passed since the disappearance of the last Imam. In every generation, overseeing the legitimacy of those claiming descent from this Family has been the responsibility of the "Naqib of the Nobility." This title naqib is at the same time shared by leaders in the orders of Islamic chivalry as well as by those saints forming a particular rank called the Nuqaba'; according to Shaykh Muhyiuddin Ibn al-`Arabi, these Nuqaba' are twelve in number.[23] That the twelve lions of the court in the Alhambra should be considered in the context of sanctity in Islam is suggested by the 124 columns surrounding them, since the prophets and saints are each said to number 124,000. More particularly, an inscription on the rim of the fountain's basin refers to lion warriors at the command of the caliph, and since the caliph had long been absent from the political life of Muslim Spain, the Court of Lions should be seen in light of eschatology. Within an Arthurian context, the ring of twelve lion warriors recalls the twelve Knights of the Round Table.[24]

----

[22] Compare this with the words of the Emerald Tablet: "Its father is the sun, its mother is the moon…"

[23] The title is traced principally to the Holy Qur'an (V, 12), in which the word naqib is applied to the leaders of the twelve tribes of the community of Moses. In Islamic mysticism, the stone struck by Moses with his staff and from which sprung twelve fountains is commemorated in an engrailed white stone with twelve points or rays (cf. the appendix to *The Royal Book of Spiritual Chivalry*). The stone of Moses is moreover associated with his ablutions, and at the tomb of the saint Hajji Bektash in Anatolia the ablution fountain flows from a lion-headed spout under a large example of these engrailed white stones more often worn by Sufis around their necks; at the fountain in Minas Tirith, Frodo receives the white gem to wear around his neck. The Bektashi Sufi Order reserved positions for twelve leaders in their meeting houses, and preserved many aspects of spiritual chivalry within Europe. A most remarkable example of European Bektashi art in the present context depicts a ring of twelve saints amidst the symbols of engrailed stone, lion, sword, sun and moon, and seven stars (reproduced in Frederick DeJong, "Pictorial Art of the Bektashi Order," *The Dervish Lodge: Architecture, Art, and Sufism in Ottoman Turkey*, University of California, 1992, page 233).

[24] This is especially true when considering the legendary "sleep" of these knights underneath the hills until their eschatological awakening, since according to medieval iconography, the lion embodies vigilance in its sleep with open eyes. Curiously, legends similar to those concerning the fate of Arthur and his knights are told of the last Muslim king of Granada and his knights by Washington

In *The Lord of the Rings*, it is particularly the court of King Théoden of Rohan that evokes the court of King Arthur, and not simply because of the recurrence of the number twelve in the chivalry of Rohan, both in the number of its household guard as well as in the 120 riders in the éored military unit. It is moreover in its obvious Dark Age Englishness that the Golden Hall of Théoden evokes Camelot, and just as Arthur's rule preserved the Roman order against barbarism, so does Rohan guard the marches of Gondor. Of course, Gandalf's counseling of the king suggests the role of Merlin,[25] and no doubt the king is "awakened" to return to the battlefield; but it is for a more subtle reason that the comparison is indisputable. In the legends of the Grail, the court of Arthur is distinct from the Grail castle; the knight destined to achieve the Grail enters the court of Arthur from the wilds, and after serving Camelot discovers his family at the Grail Castle and ultimately comes to rule there. Aragorn likewise emerges from the wilds of the North and first serves King Théoden[26] before reaching the Grail Castle of Minas Tirith, where after his arrival the swan banner of his kinsmen of Dol Amroth is flown for a time; and like Parzival, Aragorn attains his sovereignty in the castle only after a brief visit, departure and return.[27] And the swan banner not so subtly recalls the Knight of the Swan who belongs to the Grail family. According to Tolkien, the princes of Dol Amroth[28] represent a branch of the Númenórean Faithful, and so the identification follows that the Númenórean bloodline is equivalent in Tolkien's vision to the bloodline of the Grail family.

Following the mortal wounding of King Théoden on the battlefield, Tolkien alludes to the Fountain of Life in luminous terms:

Irving in his *Tales of the Alhambra*; the twelfth Imam has likewise been the focus of such mythic imagination in the case of Shiite Muslims.

[25] Since, as was mentioned already, Merlin as well as Gandalf-Mithrandir may be compared with Mithra, so Gandalf and Merlin may be brought into obvious correspondence.

[26] It should be noted that Éomer, the nephew of King Théoden, corresponds to Gawain, the nephew of King Arthur, especially in friendship to the Grail Knight.

[27] However, it must be admitted that the healing of the "wounded king" of the Grail family, accomplished on Parzival's return, is most nearly approximated by Aragorn's healing of the wounded Faramir during his brief visit, not his return.

[28] The name Amroth recalls at the same time the keeper of the Grail Joseph of Arimathea, and the Amrita of ancient India that bestows immortality.

...and before the dais lay Théoden King of the Mark upon a
bed of state; and twelve torches stood about it, and twelve
guards, knights both of Rohan and Gondor. And the hangings
of the bed were green and white but upon the king was laid
the great cloth of gold up to his breast...The light of the torches
shimmered in his white hair like sun in the spray of a fountain,
but his face was fair and young, save that a peace lay on it
beyond the reach of youth; and it seemed that he slept.[29]

Here the legend of Arthur's supernatural sleep[30] is evoked in Théoden's
martyrdom, yet becomes rather a foretaste of the eternal life promised by
religion.[31] Because of Théoden's attainment, he is placed in the Hallows
of Minas Tirith among the tombs of Gondor's Númenórean family, and
so near Elendil himself; his attainment is holiness, in accordance with the
meaning of "hallows."[32] Here also the formerly separate realms of Rohan
and Gondor, separate like the courts of Arthur and the Grail, are
integrated in peace at the dawning of a new age. The Arthurian
significance of the Court of the Lions suggests a similar integration for
Europe and Islam.[33]

---

[29] "The Houses of Healing." This ring of twelve at the center of the seven-walled
city relates to the ring of twelve lions at the center of the 124 columns in the court
of the Alhambra, since 1+2+4 is seven.

[30] It should not be overlooked that Avalon, where some accounts claim Arthur
was healed of his wounds, becomes in Tolkien's imagination the haven of
Avallónë at the shore of the Blessed Realm.

[31] "Think not of those who are slain in the way of God as dead. Nay, they are
living" (Qur'an III, 169). It is of interest to note that martyrs in Islam are not
washed as other corpses are, since it is believed the angels wash the bodies of the
martyrs with a superior ablution.

[32] Whereas Théoden is eventually transferred to a burial mound of Rohan,
appendix B of The Lord of the Rings relates that the Hobbits Merry and Pippin
come to be interred alongside the heir of Elendil in the Hallows of Gondor,
suggesting that belonging to the family of the Faithful is an honor not wholly
dependent on the materiality of a bloodline. On the other hand, the bloodline of
Númenor is in itself no guarantee of sanctity, as proven by the "Black
Númenórean" Ringwraith: corruptio optimi pessima, the best when corrupted
become the worst.

[33] No doubt the Christian conquest of Granada in 1492 was a wounding blow
against cultural integration, since by all accounts Jewish, Christian, and Muslim
communities were in greater harmony under Muslim rule. It is of interest to note,
however, that the Christian conquerors were nonetheless related to the Family of

In certain respects Aragorn recalls Parzival, the Christian Grail Knight, while in others, especially in his marriage to the Grail maiden, he recalls Parzival's Muslim brother Feirefiz;[34] so Tolkien has united both Muslim and Christian quests in his Grail Knight. Yet it is in special accordance with the Islamic heritage of Hermeticism that the green "Elfstone" is Tolkien's Grail, and King "Elessar" his Grail King. The restoration of the White Tree is of course emblematic of the healing of the Grail kingdom; since it is the "expected" Grail King who brings healing, his role corresponds to the worldwide role of the Mahdi in the eschatology of Islam. And green is not only the color of Paradise, to be prepared on Earth by the Mahdi; it is moreover the color that historically distinguished those belonging to the Family of the Prophet, and the Mahdi is his most noble descendant.[35] Indeed, the most distinguishing mark of Tolkien's Grail Family is the ancient legacy of the luminous

---

the Prophet through the royal family of Castile. Curiously, it was from the court of these same conquerors, and commencing in that same year, that explorers sailed west to discover the New World, a land which became associated in the minds of many – including Dr. John Dee - with Plato's Atlantis. It should further be recalled that one such explorer, Ponce de León, used the legend of the Fountain of Life to win court support for his efforts, which instead discovered riches in enslaving the Red Indians (cf. "Ponce de León and an Arab Legend," *Aramco World*, May/June 1992).

[34] Like Feirefiz and the Grail maiden, Aragorn and Arwen have a son; in the Grail legend this son is none other than the priest king Prester John, the legendary heir of the Magi who embodied a transcendent sovereignty for Medieval Europe. By the Renaissance, Prester John became identified with the Abyssinian Negus, whose Christian kingdom preserved many facets of Judaism, most remarkably in the importance accorded to the Ark of the Covenant; and what is more, in light of this religious syncretism, it is interesting that its name for the Ark derives not from the Bible but from the Holy Qur'an. In fact the Negus had sheltered a community of Muslim refugees early in the prophethood of Muhammad, whose legitimacy the Negus is said to have embraced. In the seventeenth century, the capital of this kingdom was called Gondar, a city wherein the Seal of Solomon was a favored motif.

[35] For Najmuddin Kubra, green is the color of the Pole and the descent of the Sakinah (cf. Henry Corbin, *The Man of Light in Iranian Sufism*, page 78-9). Another description of the mysterious Sakinah should be mentioned here, again related by at-Tabari, in connection with the form of the Grail described by Chrétien de Troyes: "The Sakinah is a basin of gold in which the hearts of the prophets are washed" (*The History of al-Tabari, Volume III*, page 131).

forehead which appears in various forms,[36] embodying the forms of light that are so many gleams of the transcendent Light of Muhammad, and so very like the Grail itself that was according to Wolfram a transcendent reality brought to Earth.

In the Grail legend, Parzival is expected to ask the redeeming "question" when he receives the sword of the Grail King; he is later told that although the sword will be broken, it may be reforged with the knowledge acquired from the Grail Castle in the waters of a fountain, and so "'the sword will become whole again, the joinings and edges stronger than before, and the signs engraved on the blade will not lose their shine.'"[37] It would seem that Andúril – reforged and engraved with its luminaries - is none other than this blade of the Grail King, and so Tolkien has reforged a sword which Wolfram had left broken at the conclusion of his story. J.R.R. Tolkien has without proper recognition taken up the challenge of the Grail quest, bringing the "Matter of Britain" arguably to its most profound expression. "The stone which the builders rejected has become the head of the corner," the saying of Jesus in the Bible, is not out of place here, since the Grail stone was rejected long ago by the "builders" of the Grail legend, only to be restored at last by Tolkien; and just as the legend originally took its form from the influence of spiritual chivalry, he has appropriately "completed" the Grail legend with his formulation of the Mahdi, the Seal of Spiritual Chivalry and the final achievement of the Family of the Prophet. So *The Lord of the Rings* announces that the completion of the Grail quest properly belongs to eschatology, and therefore has yet to be attained.

---

[36] Again, this light is embodied above all in the Star of Elendil diadem and on the Elven brows of Elrond's kin; yet it should be recalled that the first king of Númenor was the brother of Elrond, and so both forms of this light relate to one and the same family, that of Eärendil. And even the kissing of foreheads among the Men of the West must be included among the formulations of this legacy (cf. "Journey to the Crossroads," *The Two Towers*).

[37] *Parzival*, page 138. The symbols of lion, fountain, and broken sword all appear in *The Chemical Marriage of Christian Rosenkreutz*.

9

The Stuart and the King

Tolkien's designation of the ruler of Minas Tirith before the king's return as the "Steward" should be seen as holding great import for the Catholic author, as well as for any of the Catholic faith in Britain. For it was the house of Stuart – from "Steward" – that championed the Catholic cause in the United Kingdom, a kingdom that moreover only became "united" under Stuart rule, in the era of Dr. Dee[1] and what has been called the "Rosicrucian Enlightenment" of the early seventeenth century. Oxford at this time was a center of Rosicrucian influence in Britain, especially through the Hermeticism of Robert Fludd. However, by the middle of the seventeenth century, the last vestiges of Medieval Christendom had been abandoned, and, according to René Guénon, the initiatory integrity of the Rosicrucian tradition had been lost.[2] In Britain, Cromwell's disruption of the monarchy – indeed the only interruption in its history – belongs to this same period. And while the house of Stuart outlived this disruption into the "Restoration" of Charles II, the Stuarts were soon after eclipsed by the accession of a line of Protestant rulers with a less direct claim to royal legitimacy. In the eighteenth century,

---

[1] Since Dr. Dee has long been perceived as a model for Prospero in Shakespeare's most alchemical play, *The Tempest*, it is remarkable that a recent study of Tolkien has called Prospero a model for Gandalf (Shippey, *op. cit.*, page 196).

[2] *Perspectives on Initiation*, page 239. In this light the efforts of Sebottendorf, the "Ottoman Rosicrucian," to reform European Hermeticism appear to have been driven by a real need. It is likewise of interest to note that the reformation of American Freemasonry known as the Shriners – the "Mystic Shrine" being the Holy Ka`ba of Islam – proceeded from a link with Sufism. It may in fact be observed that the persistence with which Hermeticists have claimed an affiliation with the mysteries in Islam has more to do with initiatory integrity than with the dependence upon Islam for the transmission of Hermetic texts, since after the Middle Ages other sources for the latter had been found.

their exile gave rise to the Jacobite rebellions that sought to restore the
Stuarts to their "divine right."[3] Bonnie Prince Charlie, the son of James
III and the Princess Sobieski, was the Young Pretender to the title of
Charles III, and led his Highlanders in the last of these wars.[4] Although
his restoration remained unachieved, long did the partisans of his house
hope for his return.

The association of the Steward of Minas Tirith with the historical
Stuart dynasty is further suggested by the fact that Rome was the
ultimate location of the Stuart court in exile, where the last Pretender
became Count Albany. In a flamboyant display of "applicability,"
Tolkien has his last Steward of the White Tower married with the House
of Rohan that had adopted the Hobbit Merry or Meriadoc, when history
records that the daughter of Count Albany in Rome was mistress to the
son of Meriadec of Rohan.[5] Another way in which this association is
established is in the allegiance sworn to the Stewards by Pippin or
Peregrin Took, since among Hobbits it is the Tooks who held the office of
Thain, a title holding a very particular association with Scotland,[6] the
homeland of the Stuarts.[7] It should also be added that Shakespeare's
Macbeth has been interpreted as a tribute to the first Stuart king of Great
Britain; and the most obvious improvements Tolkien offers to the art of
Shakespeare are in reworking motifs very specific to that play which
concerns the Scottish monarchy.[8]

The original function of the Stuarts had been as stewards of the
King of Scotland. What distinguished this monarch was his coronation

[3] Christopher Tolkien has discovered Jacobite sentiments in his father's writing;
cf. for example *The War of the Ring*, pages x-xi.

[4] He was assisted on campaign by elderly companions called the "Seven Men of
Moidart."

[5] Cagliostro, one of the most infamous alchemists in European history, was
advisor to the Catholic Prince of Rohan at the time of the "Affair of the
Necklace."

[6] This detail would seem to develop from Tolkien's playful account in *The Hobbit*
of a Took ancestor having invented the game of golf in beheading the goblin
Golfimbul.

[7] Stuart rule is more exactly traced to its court in Edinburgh. Like Rome and
Constantinople, Edinburgh is situated on a site having seven hills. The authors of
On the Trail of Merlin (Aquarian, 1991) have observed that Duneadain, cited as
the original name of the city, is rather similar to Tolkien's Dúnedain.

[8] Cf. Shippey, *op. cit.*, page 193.

on the legendary "Stone of Destiny," an heirloom of the High Kings of Ireland that had passed to the Scots. Yet the Stone was further traced through Spain to the Holy Land, and was identified with Jacob's Pillow on which that prophet was granted his vision of the Heavenly Ladder,[9] and so also with the pedestal of the Ark of the Covenant in Jerusalem. Having served for centuries as the Coronation Stone of the Scottish Kings, it passed in turn to the English Kings with Edward I. At the same time, with the marriage of Edward I to Eleanor[10] of Castile, the noble Arab blood of the Family of the Prophet Muhammad is first shared with the sovereigns of Britain.

These developments were contemporary with the emergence of the Stuarts as the rulers of Scotland, with the marriage of Walter the Stewart to the daughter of King Robert the Bruce. This change in the succession is strangely tied to the legendary fate of the heart of Robert the Bruce. The King had ordered that upon his death, his heart should be removed from his body and borne in a casket for burial in Jerusalem. Thus it is related that a small company of loyal knights arrived in Spain bearing the heart to join the forces of Alfonso XI of Castile against the last army of Islam in Western Europe, that of Granada. During the conflict the heart was thrown against the army of Islam, with the words:

> Brave heart, that ever foremost led,
> Forward! As thou wast wont. And I
> Shall follow thee, or else shall die![11]

Even more strangely, the casket was later recovered from the battlefield. By a strange coincidence, the date of this conflict was 25 March, likewise the date of the Bruce's coronation; and this date was also chosen by Tolkien for the beginning of the new age in Middle-earth.[12] The recovered heart of the king was not destined for Jerusalem; rather it was returned to Scotland, yet not to be reunited with the king's body!

---

[9] This Heavenly Ladder is none other than that ascended by the Prophet Muhammad during his Night Journey.

[10] The name Elanor appears in *The Lord of the Rings* for the Hobbit child born on the day marking the new Age, who "looked more like an elf-maid than a Hobbit" (appendix B) and so embodies a sanctified bloodline.

[11] Barbour, *The Bruce*.

[12] This date is moreover of particular significance in Mithraism.

The casket was interred in the not too distant Melrose Abbey instead, a most significant location for many reasons that concern *The Lord of the Rings*. Legend holds that Michael Scot rests there with his alchemical books. Roger Bacon praised Scot's legacy. While Oxford has been claimed as his university, it is known that Scot studied in Toledo, where Wolfram von Eschenbach specifically traced his account of the Grail; indeed his learning was particularly in the language of Arabic and in the sciences of Islam. Because of his knowledge he was an advisor to the Holy Roman Emperor Frederick II, and was known throughout medieval Europe as the "Wizard." Melrose Abbey is furthermore at the base of the Eildon Hills, a legendary entrance to Elfland; descriptions of a sojourn there provided a source for Tolkien's vision of the Elven land of Lothlórien.[13] But perhaps most significant in the context of eschatology, beneath the Eildon Hills is a legendary resting place for the Once and Future King Arthur and his knights, the British image of the Qur'anic Companions of the Cave.

In this tapestry of legend, the heart of Robert the Bruce – the "vessel" containing his most royal inheritance from High Kings – is presented in relation to Islam in Western Europe, and in alliance with the very family of Castile that delivered the holy blood of the Prophet's Family to the British monarchy.[14] While the Stuarts did inherit what remained of the Bruce's bloodline, the function of a Steward is properly to serve. The transference of the Coronation Stone to join the Family of the Prophet in London suggests a reformulation of legitimacy, with which the blood of the Stuarts had to be reconciled.[15] Now this Coronation Stone is associated with the Ark of the Covenant; as described above, the appearance of the Prophet Muhammad not only fulfilled the prophetic succession depicted among the Ark's contents, but with his appearance there was more significantly a transformation in the

---

[13] Cf. Shippey, *op. cit.*, page 89.
[14] This bloodline again entered that of the English kings through the marriage of Alfonso XI's daughter.
[15] Centuries after the time of Robert the Bruce, the house of Stuart came to share in the holy blood through its marriage with English royalty, and only with that blood came to rule a United Kingdom with the "divine right" bestowed by coronation on the Stone of Destiny. Curiously, both the casket from Melrose Abbey and the Coronation Stone from London's Westminster Abbey were delivered to Edinburgh in 1996; the heart was finally reinterred, once again in Melrose, two years later.

presence of the Sakinah from the Ark to the hearts of the faithful. In the Holy Qur'an,[16] the Sakinah is mentioned as being present in the cave wherein the Prophet of Islam and his future caliph Abu Bakr as-Siddiq found refuge from their enemies on their Hijra; a most common motif in the histories of this event is that of the spider's web at the mouth of the cavern. It is therefore not insignificant that in the legends of Robert the Bruce, the event that is remembered best concerns a cave in which he likewise found refuge from his enemies, and it is said that he received the resolve to rise to his destiny through the example of the spider and its web at the mouth of the cave. And whereas the Sakinah is a reality particularly associated with the heart, it is particularly the heart of the Bruce that has become legendary. At Melrose Abbey, the proximity of the Arthurian "Companions of the Cave" places the conjunction of the heart of Stuart legitimacy with the Islamic heritage of a wizard in an eschatological context.

The reconciliation of a Steward with a Renewer at the end of an age is achieved in *The Lord of the Rings*. As Prince of Ithilien, the "Land of the Moon," Faramir the Steward comes to serve in a capacity that is lunar and therefore "passive" in relation to the ruler of the Tower of the Sun. Faramir first appears as a Ranger of Gondor, the captain of the archers that guard that realm,[17] with a cave as a refuge. Not only does Faramir possess knightly prowess; he is also described as "touched with the wisdom" of the Elves.[18] More tangibly, with his insight - called by Tolkien his "clear sight" – Faramir displays a power of faith, known in Islam as firasa.[19] Firasa means physiognomic discernment, a power by which character and situations may be judged. This power is the subject of the Tradition of the Prophet of Islam: "Beware the insight (firasa) of the believer, for indeed he sees by the light of Allah." By means of such

---

[16] IX, 40.

[17] The Royal Company of Archers in Edinburgh is still the personal guard of the monarch in Scotland, and Sir Walter Scott claimed that this green-clad company long maintained Jacobite sentiments.

[18] "The Siege of Gondor." Significantly, Faramir is the twenty-seventh Steward, and since the last of the twenty-seven chapters of the *Fusus al-Hikam* concerns that inheritance related to the Seal of Prophets, Faramir corresponds in some manner to a "Muhammadan" appearance.

[19] Curiously, in traditional Islam, the word faris signifies one with insight as well as the horseman, and it is said of Faramir that he is a master of men and horses alike.

vision, Faramir is able to warn Frodo the Ring-bearer at their parting, for Frodo soon after encounters the evil spider Shelob. The contrasting of the cave of Faramir and the tunnel of Shelob suggests a literary "webbing," bringing into thematic association Faramir and the spider, while providing another example of the Dark Lord's parody, in this case of the caves and beneficent spiders just mentioned. More exactly, Tolkien reinforces the association with Robert the Bruce, in calling Faramir "brave heart" on the battlefield.

Recently, attention has come to focus on the Stuart dynasty in connection with the heresy of a "Holy Bloodline," and the Grail has perhaps not surprisingly been claimed as its emblem. It is in the nature of parody that the orthodoxy of the Family of the Prophet of Islam should be imitated by the heresy of a bloodline of kings descending from Jesus, with the evidence of the Grail family forced to support its will-o'-the-wisp assertions. With the absence of the royal dimension in the foundation of Christianity, and the theological conflation of God and Jesus in later Christian doctrine, this heresy has embraced the notion of a "God-King." It is remarkable that Tolkien's imagination should not only establish so explicitly the Antichristic significance of the "God-king" Sauron,[20] but that the bloodline of the Faithful should be identified by such distinctively Muhammadan signs as the Star of Elendil, the sword and the black banner.[21] Two alternatives are presented for the Stewards of Minas Tirith upon the return of the rightful king whose blood has the greatest share of Númenórean legitimacy: the Steward may serve in wisdom in accordance with the example of Faramir, or the Steward may

---

[20] According to Tolkien, "Sauron desired to be a God-King, and was held to be this by his servants; if he had been victorious he would have demanded divine honor from all rational creatures and absolute temporal power over the whole world" (*Letters*, number 183).

[21] The Prophet Muhammad is called Owner of the Crown, Staff (identified above as the sword) and Banner. Concerning the designation "Elendili" for the Faithful, the name Elendil is composed of three Elvish letters, "which he used as a badge, and a device upon his seals" ("Cirion and Eorl"). The first and last of these letters are both lambe, and flank the middle letter ando that carries the significance of "gate;" the lambe, curiously, is identical in form to the Arabic letter ج. So this device at the source of the bloodline of the Faithful may be related to the designations for the two streams of the bloodline of the Prophet, Hasani and Husayni, that begin with the very same Arabic letter. Al-Mahdi is both Hasani and Husayni in his lineage from the Prophet Muhammad.

assume an authority like the "'heathen kings, under the domination of the Dark Power,'"[22] and so find an infernal doom, like Denethor, whose pyre violates the Hallows of the bloodline of Númenor.

The heresy of the "bloodline of Jesus" is no doubt a facet of what Guénon identified as the Counter-tradition,[23] and it is not insignificant that this heresy should offer a Stuart prince as a rival for the throne of Great Britain. Nevertheless, the true heir to this throne, the present Great Steward of Scotland and Prince of Wales,[24] Charles Philip Arthur George, whose birth was contemporary with the writing of The Lord of the Rings, is ready to become King Charles III or King Arthur II in the achievement of a long hoped for renewal.[25] He is not only from the Family of the Prophet; through his father HRH the Duke of Edinburgh, he is said to be related to the Shahs of Persia.[26] Prince Charles' heirs inherit an even greater share in the Stuart bloodline through their mother Princess Diana.[27]

HRH the Prince of Wales has proven himself a brave horseman, especially in the sport of Polo that historically derives from the practice of princes in Islam. He has also proven his insight in many fields, notably in his defense of traditional cosmological principles in architecture; and a most remarkable proof was his speech at Oxford on Islam and the West:

> The contribution of Muslim Spain to the preservation of classical learning during the Dark Ages, and to the first flowerings of the Renaissance, has long been recognized...Not only did Muslim Spain gather and preserve the intellectual content of ancient Greek and Roman civilization, it also

---

[22] "The Pyre of Denethor," The Return of the King.

[23] Cf. The Reign of Quantity and the Signs of the Times.

[24] Tolkien incorporated many Welsh linguistic elements in his creation of Elvish.

[25] In this connection, it is remarkable that The Lord of the Rings as a work of literature belongs to the reign of HM Elizabeth II, and so to a second Elizabethan age, just as the plays of Shakespeare belonged to the first.

[26] This line of royalty was anciently held to enjoy a Divine Favor or Glory, called "farr;" and since "amir" is Arabic for "prince," the name Faramir translates literally as "Princely Glory."

[27] Diana's affair with a wealthy Egyptian ended in their doom against a column in a Paris street tunnel; by a strange coincidence, the name of the Egyptian was Imaduddin, the "Column" of Religion.

interpreted and expanded upon that civilization, and made a vital contribution of its own in so many fields of human endeavor...

More than this, Islam can teach us today a way of understanding and living in the world which Christianity itself is the poorer for having lost...What I am appealing for is a wider, deeper, more careful understanding of our world; for a metaphysical as well as material dimension to our lives, in order to recover the balance we have abandoned, the absence of which, I believe, will prove disastrous in the long term...[28]

And in reference to the title "Defender of the (Anglican) Faith" that he would inherit, the Prince has moreover declared his hope to serve in a rather more profound way as a Defender of Faith: "I would much rather it was seen as defending faith itself which is so often under threat in our day."[29]

---

[28] Lecture given in the Sheldonian Theatre, Oxford on 27 October 1993. The reference to the "balance" recalls the alchemical doctrine of Jabir Ibn Hayyan.
[29] Jonathan Dimbleby, *The Prince of Wales*, William Morrow, 1994, page 528. Cf. pages 307-08 for the relationship between HRH and the alchemist Paracelsus.

78

10

The White Tower

Like the Philosopher's Stone and the legendary Grail, the veneration of the Virgin Mary belongs both to Christianity and Islam. Indeed, the Cult of the Virgin only came to dominate Catholicism with the Age of Chivalry, which is the age of encounter with Islam that likewise produced the Grail legends.[1] As Tolkien himself admitted, perhaps the clearest expression of Catholic religiosity in his work is the example of the Elven Lady Galadriel.[2] Although very little explicitly identifies Galadriel with the Virgin Mary, there can be little doubt that both in the love and devotion she inspires as well as in her intercessionary role, the "White Lady" appears in the image of the Virgin. Concerning the alchemical work, the stage called the "whitening" is particularly associated in Christendom with the Blessed Virgin. Even though Arwen Evenstar had come to possess the Elfstone, it was originally associated with the White Lady, and it is indeed from her hand that Aragorn receives it. Not only does this particular transmission preclude the suggestion that the Elfstone is given as some romantic token, but it more especially recalls the bestowal of the rank of "Knight of the Golden Stone" to the legendary founder of the Rosicrucians by the Virgin.

The White Lady's appearance in the story appropriately follows the "blackening" of Moria;[3] her distinctive emblem, the Mirror of

---

[1] As if in confirmation of her sanctity in the context of Islam is the subsequent appearance of the Virgin as Our Lady of Fatima, since Fatima is the name of the Prophet's daughter.

[2] Cf. *Letters*, especially numbers 143 and 320.

[3] That Moria is a "mine" recalls the teaching of Morienus to the king Khalid on the matter of Alchemy: "This thing is extracted from you, for you are its mine." The similarity of the names "Moria" and "Morienus" need hardly be mentioned.

Galadriel, is prefigured in the Mirrormere pool – with its reflections like "white flame" - that is reached immediately upon emerging from Moria, and so both "mirrors" are also waters. What is revealed in the "whitening" is known as the Materia Prima, both feminine and lunar, that in its capacity to hold all the possibilities of formal manifestation is indeed best symbolized by either waters[4] or the mirror. What is more, the clear mirror of the soul that is reached beyond "death" contrasts with the dark and unclean depths of the soul before the alchemical transmutation.[5] Remarkably, these depths are embodied in the unclean pool standing outside the entrance to Moria that is the home of the monstrous "Watcher in the Water," a designation that parodies Galadriel's use of her mirror. The White Lady herself comments upon the failure of language alone – or at least the English language - to discriminate between the reality of her mirror and its parody: "'For this is what your folk would call magic,[6] I believe; though I do not understand clearly what they mean; and they seem also to use the same word of the deceits of the Enemy.'"[7]

Burkhardt notes that a book containing the teachings of Morienus was perhaps the first book on Alchemy to be translated into Latin from Arabic.

[4] This aspect of the Materia Prima would seem to be evoked by the King at his coronation, in the phrase "out of the Great Sea." The watery purification of Isengard may also be related to an alchemical "solve."

[5] The need for the alchemical "death" is expressed in the command of the Prophet of Islam: "Die before you die."

[6] It is, of course, from the Persian "magi" that the word "magic" is derived.

[7] "The Mirror of Galadriel." The divinatory "Mirror of Galadriel" recalls the report of the historian Ibn Khaldun on the ability of the `arraf to use mirrors or pools of water for unlawful divination. Yet the word `arraf is from the root meaning "to perceive" or "to recognize," and so is related to the name of the chapter of the Holy Qur'an called al-A`raf, and thus incidentally to the poem by Edgar Allen Poe of the same name. The name of this chapter refers to saints with the power of insight: "And on the Heights are men who recognize them all by their marks. And they call unto the dwellers of the Garden: Peace be unto you! They enter it not, although they hope (to enter)" (VII, 46). While the power of insight has already been associated with the wisdom of the Elves, it is remarkable that these Watchers from the Heights have not yet joined the dwellers of the Garden, just as the Elves of Middle-earth yet hope to make the journey to Aman. The Ottoman chronicler Evliya Efendi moreover describes the fantastic use of a divinatory pool of water by a saintly elite (cf. "Narrative of Gul-ábí Aghá" in Hammer-Purgstall's translation).

The author of *Parzival* composed his story on the basis of realities which bring Christianity and Islam together. Wolfram von Eschenbach attributed his "true story" to a mysterious figure named Flegetanis who had discovered the legend of the Grail in the stars. In reality, this name designates one of the levels of Heaven, specifically the second Heaven (falak ath-thani) that is under the authority of Jesus in the cosmology of Islam.[8] Now, this level is that of the planet Mercury, the Roman form of Hermes, and so the relationship between the second Heaven and that of the sun demands some explanation, since the Hermetic sciences are explicitly related to Idris. Above all, Mercury is associated with the art of healing, and Jesus was a healer in the most profound sense.[9] While Alchemy is an application of the Hermetic sciences, it is specifically the "royal art," and the absence of the royal aspect from the historical example of Jesus, as mentioned above, distinguishes that role from the solar function at the center of the cosmos which must in its position of unity include the royal dimension.[10]

The true account of the Grail, then, from its inspiration in Flegetanis or the Islamic Heaven of Jesus, offers the Christian world guidance from Islamic sources concerning those royal arts absent from the historical Christian revelation. Of course, the separation of the cosmological sciences and chivalry from the Hermetic ideals of *Parzival* has brought the perversion both of modern science and the arts of warfare. In a very real sense, *The Lord of the Rings* is a response to the evils of scientific industrialization and the World Wars corrupting Tolkien's England. Its restoration of a chivalry expressed in the language of Alchemy not surprisingly uncovers a relationship with Islam, due to its continuation of the Hermetic Grail legend. There is, however, an important distinction to be made, in that *The Lord of the Rings* concerns very precisely the Solar domain of Idris, not that of "Flegetanis."

René Guénon has quite rightly observed that "it would seem then that the two comings of Christ may be related to his 'Mercurial' and

---

[8] Cf. Ponsoye, *op. cit.*, page 26.

[9] The caduceus, of course, is most well known as the symbol of the healing profession, since health is also wholeness. In Islam, the prophet Idris is the originator of the physician's craft, and very many others.

[10] It is appropriate, then, that Idris is regarded in Islam as a teacher of the martial arts.

'Solar' aspects;"[11] for indeed it is in the Second Coming of Jesus that his role is completed with the restoration of the royal aspect to his Heavenly authority.[12] Mention was already made to the role of Idris as the cosmic deputy of the light or reality of Muhammad at the level of the sun, a role which corresponds to that of Mitatrun among the angels.[13] Not surprisingly, then, the Second Coming means the return of Jesus to confirm in his "Solar" aspect the reality of Muhammad in one of the greatest eschatological signs of Islam. In the Traditions of Islamic eschatology, Jesus descends from Heaven "supported on the wings of two angels" as the followers of the Mahdi are preparing to pray, and although the leadership of the prayer is offered to the son of Mary, he insists on following and so declares his belonging to the community of the Prophet Muhammad. Upon seeing Jesus, the Antichrist begins to dissolve "like salt dissolves in water," and the prophet then manifests his knightly power in slaying the Antichrist, and "shows his blood on his spear." The age that follows is properly a Golden Age, a worldwide "Kingdom of Heaven on Earth," under his rule.

Here *The Lord of the Rings* seems to depart from its eschatological significance, for if the Dark Lord Sauron evokes the Antichrist, and the heir of the King of the Faithful the Mahdi, there is no obvious candidate for the eschatological role of Jesus; and while it could be said that it is Frodo the Ring-bearer who unmakes the evil of the Dark Lord, his character is more in accordance with the historical example of Jesus, especially since he ultimately abandons Middle-earth for the "paradise" of Aman. What is more, it should not be overlooked that in the identification of the Elfstone with the Mahdi, Tolkien's work does not follow the routine equating of Christ with the Philosopher's Stone in the conception of Christian alchemists. To understand this apparent departure from eschatology is not too difficult, since *The Lord of the Rings* is presented as a history of ancient legend, and the future descent of Jesus is for a Christian like Tolkien far too unique an event to be even

---

[11] "Hermes," *op. cit.*, page 374 note 8. That the apostles of Jesus number twelve should be recognized as a prefiguring of this solar aspect.

[12] Indeed Jesus is considered one of the Awtad in Islamic mysticism whose role, like that of al-Khidr, has a perennial aspect.

[13] Mitatrun is at the center of the four archangels like the Prophet Muhammad is at the center of his four Rightly-guided Caliphs. This position is called in Arabic the Rukn al-arkan, "mystery of mysteries," and returns to the significance of five.

approximated. Through the events that are depicted, the Hobbits are the focus of the reader's sympathies, and Gandalf provides a reason for those events upon their return to their homeland of the Shire: "'I am not coming to the Shire. You must settle its affairs yourselves; that is what you have been trained for…and I have no longer any fear at all for any of you.'"[14] Since the descent of Jesus is final, there can be no struggle to follow, and "The Scouring of the Shire" is offered as an inspiration for those who must in the end leave the pages of Middle-earth and struggle in the world. Yet the very absence of the eschatological role of Jesus in the Christian author's vision of the end of an age leaves the reader looking for that reality.

Yet there is one sign which points clearly to that reality, once again in the geography of Gondor. At the summit of the city of Minas Anor is the White Tower, a designation that recalls very remarkably a Tradition describing the descent of Jesus: according to the Prophet of Islam, "Jesus the son of Mary will descend at the White Tower of Damascus." For this reason, attention must be given to that tower of the Damascus mosque in Syria, and even though its location is far from Rome, the word "Syria" has long identified the "Land of the Sun,"[15] and so approximates Tolkien's Anor. Louis Massignon has moreover illuminated a remarkable connection between Rome and Damascus concerning the development of the veneration of the Companions of the Cave in both cities.[16] The city of Damascus is a land of saints, the headquarters of the Abdal, and the resting place of the Great Master Muhyiuddin Ibn al-`Arabi. It is counted amongst the strongholds of safety against the Dajjal or Antichrist; similarly, the city of Minas Tirith is literally the Tower of Guard against the forces of Sauron.

The heritage of the White Tower of Damascus is related in an account by Masoudi: "The Damascus Mosque was a huge temple before Christianity. This temple…was dedicated to Mercury, the Star of Good Fortune. When Christianity arrived, the temple became a church. Then Islam appeared and it became a mosque which was later rebuilt by (the caliph). The towers did not change and they serve as the minarets for the

---

[14] "Homeward Bound," *The Return of the King*. Again, in the Holy Qur'an, the saints are those "on whom there is no fear."

[15] Cf. Guénon, "The Science of Letters," *Fundamental Symbols of Sacred Science*.

[16] Damascus is also where the legendary founder of the Rosicrucians received his initiation into the mysteries.

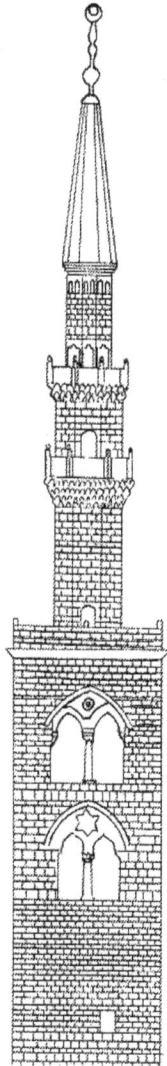

The White Tower, or Jesus Minaret

muezzin until now." Not only is its Hermetic identification remarkable in the present context, but for a time, both Christians and Muslims worshipped in the same building. In its rebuilding, the primary construction was called the Dome of the Eagle. And very significant indeed is that on every side of the White Tower, called also the Jesus Minaret, is a window in the stone of the tower in the shape of the Seal of Solomon.[17]

The descent of Jesus at the White Tower of Damascus follows after the appearance of the Mahdi and the marshalling of his followers against the Dajjal. Indeed the role of the Mahdi is in a sense to prepare the faithful for that descent. The prophet Elias has long been expected to prepare the descent of the Messiah, and it has been observed that the Mahdi fulfills in this sense an "Eliatic function."[18] Concerning this eschatological formulation of the Eliatic function, a Tradition relates that it is for the Mahdi that "the Earth will bring forth what is hidden from its depths which look like cylinders of gold and silver;" this mysterious and alchemical image compares very remarkably with the alchemical expectation of Elias Artista, about whom it was foretold that "there shall be nothing so hidden that it shall not be revealed." What is more, the Damascus Mosque is the resting place of the head of John the Baptist, and so in this location sacred to Christianity and Islam converge two formulations of this Eliatic function, relating respectively to the historical and eschatological appearances of Jesus. In *The Lord of the Rings*, the role of Elias Artista is identified with the Eliatic function of the Mahdi, and in recognizing this identification the return of the King of the Faithful to the White Tower becomes a kind of preparation, embodying in Tolkien's imaginary history the promise made by Jesus in the Gospel of Matthew: "Elias truly shall first come, and restore all things."

In the last pages of *The Lord of the Rings*, Tolkien brings his alchemy to completion; as already mentioned, this completion is associated with the color red, and so is the stage of "reddening." Not until the end does Tolkien reveals the ruby ring of Gandalf, even though the wizard always had this "red" talisman in his possession, as appendix B confirms. Similarly, in the last appearance of King Elessar, Tolkien depicts the "reddening:" "they saw the King of the West sitting upon his

---

[17] Here the symbol's two triangles particularly signify the "two natures" of Jesus, called in Islamic mysticism the lahut (divine) and the nasut (human).
[18] Cf. Leo Schaya, *op. cit.*

horse with his knights about him; and the falling Sun shone upon them and made all their harness to gleam like red gold, and the white mantle of Aragorn was turned to a flame."[19] But most explicit is the "reddening" that belongs to the Ring-bearers Bilbo and Frodo, the "Red Book of Westmarch." Composed for the most part in Imladris, this red book is the record of the story begun in *The Hobbit* and brought to perfection in *The Lord of the Rings*; more exactly, it is titled "The Downfall of the Lord of the Rings and the Return of the King," and so reformulates the alchemical expression "solve et coagula."[20] For Tolkien the scholar, Alchemy is contained first and foremost in the contents of a book.

Indeed the science of Alchemy in Islam is bound up with what is called the "Science of Letters," in which everything in existence is related to its archetype through the hidden significance of letters. In Islamic sources, Hermes, Pythagoras, Plato, and Aristotle were all teachers of this science. In the Middle Ages, Christian scholars sought to uncover its secrets from Islamic sources; in particular, the study of the derivative science of geomancy was called the study of the abc's because of its foundation in the "Science of Letters."[21] According to the Great Master

---

[19] "Many Partings."

[20] These formulations may even be related to the "testimony of faith" that is a pillar of Islam and a litany in the dhikr of Sufism: la ilaha ill Allah, Muhammadu Rasulullah. The first phrase negates all that is false and destroys all parodies of lordship, and the second affirms the embodiment of the light of transcendence in the King of the Prophets. The negation in the first phrase may be compared with Tolkien's description of the monotheism of the Men of the West as a negative truth: "the refusal to worship any 'creature'" (*Letters*, number 156).

[21] The Arabic name of geomancy is raml, and so it should be mentioned that in appendix E of *The Lord of the Rings*, Tolkien credits the formation of the first Elvish letters to Rúmil. Indeed, in several respects the usage of the Elvish letters recalls that of Arabic in the "Science of Letters," for example in the numbering of letters and in the preeminence of consonants over vowels (vowels being depicted with signs over the consonants, or not at all). In connection with the numerical value of Arabic letters, it should be mentioned that the number 111 – a prominent number in the first chapter of *The Lord of the Rings* – corresponds to the word qutb or Pole, and so announces the importance of that function in the whole story. The Golem of Medieval Jewish Kabbalism is an example of the magical use of letters; however, "it is related to ideas current in non-Jewish circles concerning the creation of an alchemical man" (Gershom Scholem, *Kabbalah*, Meridian, 1978, page 353). Tolkien's evoking of the term with the "wicked" Gollum does not favor a Kabbalistic interpretation. It is of interest,

Muhyiuddin Ibn al-`Arabi, who is very significantly also called the "Son of Plato," this science is the special knowledge of Jesus, and so Tolkien's explanation of *The Lord of the Rings* as "primarily linguistic in inspiration" should not be discounted, since Jesus was the focus of Tolkien's Christian belief. Not surprisingly, the revelation of the "Science of Letters" belongs especially to eschatology. According to al-Qashani's commentary on the Holy Qur'an, and relating particularly to the mysterious "isolated letters" that open certain chapters, there is a book which will descend by the command of Jesus at the end of time; its manifestation will "on the one hand reveal the Archetypes or Metaphysics, and on the other hand operate the eschatological or Messianic event;" and this book that belongs to the special knowledge of Jesus will be read and its contents explained by the Mahdi alone.[22] Still, for Muhyiuddin, known also as the "Red Sulphur" which brings transmutation, Jesus is the Alchemist. His alchemy no doubt is glimpsed in the Tradition relating the dissolving of the Imposter like salt in water, a "solve" which must precede the "coagula" of the Golden Age.[23] In Christianity and Islam, the transmutation of the greater world waits for him.

---

however, to note that the first textual mention in Judaism of the "Shield of David," a name for the Seal of Solomon in all likelihood deriving from Islamic influence, concerned an "alphabet of the angel Metatron" (*ibid.*, page 365).

[22] Quoted in Schaya, *op. cit.*

[23] This process is prefigured in the initiatory drink of salted water in spiritual chivalry.

11

Chain of Gold

Concerning the alchemical knowledge of Jesus formulated in the "Science of Letters," a special importance belongs to the command kun or "be!" In Arabic this word returns to a root of three letters: kaf, waw[1], and nun. Here is an expression of the alchemical "three times three," in this case, three letters the names of which are likewise composed of three letters, so again the significance of nine appears. In *The Lord of the Rings*, this number designates alternatively a reality and its inverse. Nine are the ships of the Faithful, and so nine relates to the nobility of the Men of the West; the inverse of this nobility is also nine-fold, in the Ringwraiths who were lords among men, led by a renegade "Black Númenórean." Again, the Nine Ringwraiths are opposed by the Nine Companions of the Fellowship of the Ring. And the evil of the Dark Lord Sauron, whose finger had been lost with his Ring, is finally undone by Frodo of the Nine Fingers. The celebration of the Nine Fingers takes place at the Field of Cormallen, and so the "circle of gold." Indeed nine is a number geometrically expressed in the circle,[2] and the arrangement of nine points in a circle gives rise to the design known as the Enneagram.[3]

---

[1] Guénon has noted that the letter waw is the "conjunctive" letter, and indeed here it serves to unite the kaf and nun. The numerical value of this letter is 6, and the Seal of Solomon is, of course, the figuration of this same number. It is tempting to suggest that the development of the solitary waw in Ottoman calligraphy, both monumental and talismanic, arose in compensation for the contemporary development of the Seal as a more and more exclusively Jewish emblem.

[2] So the circle is conventionally divided into nine-fold degrees, that is, 90, 180, 360.

[3] On the Field of Cormallen, the arrangement of three thrones recalls the triangle of three points that is essential to the pattern of the Enneagram.

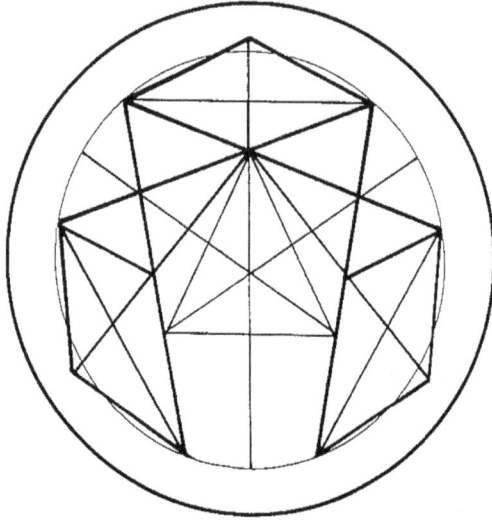

The Sufi Enneagram[4]

This design has recently been adapted into the domain of psychology, and especially by Catholics in their efforts towards a religious psychology; so the nine points refer to aspects of the personality (significantly either positive or negative) with Jesus embodying the perfection of the soul. Yet even though its origin may be traceable to ancient Pythagorean geometry, J.G. Bennett has established that the Enneagram belongs to the heritage of Islamic mysticism, and that of the Naqshbandi Order in particular. In this context, the Enneagram assumes a more profound significance with the nine points being loci of spiritual

---

[4] Dr. Laleh Bakhtiar has explained many aspects of this version of the Enneagram, especially in her *Moral Healer's Handbook: The Psychology of Spiritual Chivalry* (*God's Will Be Done Volume II*, The Institute of Traditional Psychoethics and Guidance, 1994).

inspiration, and so the design becomes "the figure of the 'Heart of the World,' the most interior place, where the great Presence of the Sakinah descends."[5]

The Prophet of Islam and Abu Bakr as-Siddiq are at the source of the initiatic chain of the Naqshbandi Order of Sufism, a chain established with the descent of the Sakinah in the cave wherein the two friends found refuge on the Hijra.[6] This order was first called the "Siddiqiyyun," after the best friend and first caliph of the Prophet Muhammad. All other Sufi orders trace their many lineages back to `Ali, the fourth caliph of the Prophet, the first Imam of his Family, the wielder of the sword Dhul-Fiqar. The initiatic chain of the Naqshbandi Order passes through the Imam Ja`far As-Sadiq, and since he received the lights from both transmissions, the Naqshbandi lineage is known as the Golden Chain. The Imam As-Sadiq was also the spiritual master of the alchemist Jabir Ibn Hayyan.[7]

This Chain of Gold is the only chain to be traced back to the first caliph, and so its inheritance may be understood as preeminently caliphal, in the sense of representing the unity of spiritual authority and royal power that belongs to the Holy Prophet. Such a significance belongs to the title Siddiqiyyun, since it is represented in the Heavenly order by Idris, called Siddiq in the Holy Qur'an. In time the Siddiqiyyun became known as the Khwajagan, the Masters of Wisdom, a title formerly used in the hierarchy of the ancient Persian court. Indeed, J.G. Bennett perceived in these Masters of Wisdom a function that he traces throughout the ages and identifies especially with the Magi of Persia, and so quotes Porphyry's definition of "magus" as "one who is wise in the things of God and serves the divine."[8] In fact, the successor of Abu Bakr as-Siddiq in the Golden Chain, Salman the Persian, had been

---

[5] Translated from Philippe de Vos, *La Genèse de la Sagesse ou la chaîne initiatique chez les Maîtres Soufis*, Dervy, 1995, page 154.

[6] "...When they were in the cave, he said unto his companion: Grieve not. Lo! Allah is with us. Then Allah caused His Sakinah to descend upon him and supported him with hosts ye could not see..." (*Qur'an*, IX, 40). This reassurance may be compared with Aragorn's leadership in the cavernous Paths of the Dead.

[7] Chodkiewicz mentions the curious fact that the first documented appearance of the term "sufi" was applied to Jabir Ibn Hayyan (*op. cit.*, page 27).

[8] *The Masters of Wisdom*, Bennett Books, 1995, page 51. It is of interest to note that in ancient China, Westerners with pointed hats served as court advisors, and were identified by a word derived from the Persian term.

brought up in the religion of the Magi before his conversion to Christianity[9] and, later still, his quest for the Prophet Muhammad and acceptance of Islam. It was in honor of Salman that the Prophet is reported to have said, "If faith were at the Pleiades, even then some men from these people (like Salman) would attain it." Even more especially, the Prophet honored him by declaring, "Salman is included among the people of my Family."[10]

By the high Middle Ages the Order of the Khwajagan was established in the center of Asia, at the crossroads of the medieval world between East and West now called the Silk Road. The Bektashi Order that during the same period reached well into Europe is considered a branch of the Khwajagan.[11] Included in the ranks of the Masters of Wisdom is al-Khidr, named in the Golden Chain Abul-`Abbas, who reached the Fountain of Life when Alexander the Great could not.[12] The order later came to bear the name of the great master who was called Shah, or King, Naqshband. But perhaps the caliphal inheritance of the Golden Chain was most apparent in the master called the "Crown Prince of Turkestan," Khwaja Ahrar. Religious authorities and royalty alike recognized in him their superior in both domains. This great Khwaja is reported to have said,

> Allah (Exalted is He) has endowed me with such strength that,
> if I wished, I could write a letter to the Emperor of China, who
> lays claim to divinity, and charm him into forsaking his throne
> and running in rags and tatters to my doorstep. Yet, even with

---

[9] The Three Wise Men who followed a star to confirm the legitimacy of the historical Jesus in Christian legend were Magi.

[10] Again, like in the Tradition of the Prophet's "brothers," such an honor seems not to depend only upon a material bloodline.

[11] The founders of the Bektashi Order became the patron saints of the Ottoman Janissaries. One of these saints, known as Sari Saltiq, established his spiritual presence in seven different locations throughout Europe and even in Scandinavia, with each location identified as his tomb. For the Ottomans, his spiritual presence subsequently became identified with St. Nicholas in the lands of the "Romans." In *The Father Christmas Letters*, Tolkien celebrates the spirit of St. Nicholas as Father Christmas, who famously resides in a very significant location, the North Pole.

[12] Significantly, the fullest collection of histories of the Masters of Wisdom was titled *Rashahat `ain al-hayat*, or "Droplets of the Fountain of Life."

such strength and power at my disposal, I am waiting for
Allah's commandment in this regard...

Very remarkably, it is known that Khwaja Ahrar was taught by the spirit
of Jesus, who may likewise be said to be "waiting for Allah's
commandment" as regards the manifestation of his eschatological
power. Nevertheless, the sun was seen to wait in the western sky for
Khwaja Ahrar to reach his destination through the wastes of Central
Asia on horseback. At the time of his passing from this life, a radiant
light was seen to shine upon his forehead.[13] With his spiritual connection
to Jesus, as well as a physical connection to his predecessor in the Golden
Chain, Khwaja Ahrar belongs to a special rank in the Naqshbandi Order:
"They are known as the shaykhs of the Two Wings, meaning that both
the physical lineage and the spiritual lineage are combined in them.
These saints are only nine in number. Each one represents one of the
nine spiritual points on the chest of the human being."[14]

While J.G. Bennett claimed to have had a spiritual connection
with Khwaja Ahrar, he physically met with the contemporary inheritor
of the Chain of Gold in Damascus. This was the Shaykh `Abdullah
Daghestani, recognized as the Sultan ul-Awliya, or the Sultan of Saints,
whose physical power reflected this royal title, and who lived well past
100 years. Not only does the master of the Golden Chain embody the
role of Siddiq; here the title of Sultan recalls especially the cosmic
authority of Idris, since it is but another designation of the supreme
polar function. Shaykh `Abdullah's tomb is located on the mountain that
dominates the city of Damascus, between a mosque dedicated to the
Abdal and the tomb of the Great Master Muhyiuddin.[15] Indeed, like

---

[13] Quote and accounts from the *Rashahat `ain al-hayat* by Mawlana `Ali Ibn
Husain Safi (translated by Muhtar Holland, Al-Baz, 2001). The author of this
classic is the son of the author of *The Royal Book of Spiritual Chivalry*. A later
account claimed that the Ottoman conquest of Constantinople was due to the
spiritual influence of Khwaja Ahrar.

[14] Shaykh Muhammad Hisham Kabbani, *The Naqshbandi Sufi Way: The History and
Guidebook of the Saints of the Golden Chain*, Kazi, 1995, page 11. This teaching
unites the microcosm and macrocosm in a perspective which is preeminently
Hermetic.

[15] It should perhaps be mentioned that the Great Master is not included in
established lines of spiritual transmission; the influence of his teachings,
however, has distinguished the Naqshbandi Order especially. What is more, the

Muhyiuddin, Shaykh `Abdullah was identified with the alchemical designation, the "Red Sulphur" among saints. Bennett describes his meeting with Shaykh `Abdullah in his book *Witness*, and relates the message he was given concerning the wickedness of the world and the "Messenger" who will come to the West[16] to show the way out of this situation.

According to religious eschatology, such a situation presages a rectification. In the words of René Guénon, "this rectification will have to be prepared, even visibly, before the end of the present cycle; but this can only be done by one who, by uniting in himself the powers of Heaven and Earth, of East and West, will manifest outwardly, both in the domain of knowledge and in that of action, the twin sacerdotal and royal power that has been preserved across the ages in the integrity of its unique principle by the hidden keepers of the primordial tradition."[17] Not until the time of Shaykh `Abdullah were the names of the seven wazirs of the Mahdi made known by the Masters of the Golden Chain, even though it had long been expected that "al-Mahdi will be one of the followers of this way."[18]

Before his passing in September 1973 – the same month as Professor Tolkien – the Sultan of Saints ordered his successor and fortieth Master of the Golden Chain, Shaykh Nazim al-Haqqani,[19] to guide the people of the West. So ever since Shaykh Nazim has traveled far and tirelessly, with frequent and prolonged stays in England, to attract an ever-growing group from many different origins. In his tall and pointed hat, long beard, flowing robes, and walking staff, there is no doubt that the appearance of this Master of the Golden Chain in England

---

Amir `Abdul Qadir, a deputy of a master of the Golden Chain, was taught directly by the spirit of Shaykh Muhyiuddin (Cf. Chodkiewicz, *The Spiritual Writings of Amir `Abd al-Kader*, SUNY, 1995).

[16] Recall the "angelic" function of Gandalf as a messenger to the West of Middle-earth.

[17] Guénon, *Perspectives on Initiation*, page 254.

[18] Shaykh Muhammad Hisham Kabbani, *op. cit.*, page 237.

[19] Prior to his mastery of the spiritual sciences, Shaykh Nazim attained a degree in the study of Chemistry, that is, the last remnant of Alchemy in the secular sciences. His land of origin is the island of Cyprus.

recalls the English conception of a wizard.[20] Already Tolkien's Wizards have been shown to evoke the wise men of Persia. More explicitly, Saruman is called "sharku" or "old man" by his followers, and this is an approximation of "shaykh" in Arabic that has the very same meaning. Here again is an example of a reality which Saruman perverts, whereas Gandalf, likewise an "old man" in appearance, affirms that: "'Indeed I *am* Saruman, one might almost say, Saruman as he should have been.'"[21] Concerning the staff that is the instrument of authority of the Wizards of Middle-earth, it is significant that a distinctive heirloom of the Khwajagan was the staff of Salman the Persian.

Shaykh Nazim is known as a Saint of the Two Wings, being a descendant and inheritor both of the Sufi master 'Abdul Qadir Jilani, himself a pure descendant of the Family of the Prophet, and of the Sufi Mevlana Jalaluddin Rumi. In the holy places associated with Mevlana Rumi, both Christian and Muslim pieties converge, and curiously also with the shared legacy of Plato;[22] this may be compared with the Hermetic heritage of the mosque in Damascus. His title Rumi - "the Roman" - derives from the association of his adopted Anatolia with the culture of East Rome; his specialty was in guiding the "Roman" or "Western" people.[23] Still, a further acceptance of Islam by the people of "Rome" is an eschatological expectation, often mentioned in light of the formula of the "Sun rising in the West;" and according to the Traditions, the good qualities of the people of "Rome" are qualities found only in the faithful.

In a talk delivered at Oxford University, Shaykh Nazim described the nature of the times in terms that resonate with Tolkien's vision of the waning of the Third Age:

---

[20] It should be acknowledged that when Gandalf is told that he is "'mighty in wizardry,'" he replies, "'That may be. But if so, I have not shown it yet. I have but given good counsel in peril…'" ("The Road to Isengard").

[21] "The White Rider."

[22] Cf. Hasluck, *op. cit.* The relationship between the legacy of Plato as formulated in Renaissance Europe and contemporary Ottoman traditions deserves a separate study.

[23] In Constantinople, the successors of Mevlana Rumi have had the distinction of girding the Ottoman caliphs with the sword of investiture, in a ceremony attended by the Naqib of the Nobility.

It is through science that devils are now controlling everything of mankind. Only heavenly knowledge brings peace. Mankind is now refusing heavenly knowledge. They are refusing peace. They will never find peace on earth if they don't take it from heavenly books, from heavenly knowledge...It is mentioned, that when the last days are coming and the Day of Resurrection is approaching on earth, the good-quality-people will lose control of the world and the control will be in the hands of worst-quality-people who are against anything heavenly, that is: everything that has been mentioned in the Old, New, and Last Testament[24]...I'm sorry to say, that mostly people will become handles of destruction to destroy our original characteristics, original attributes and noble customs that we inherited from our ancestors, especially here in England. They say, "It's old fashioned. We need new fashions, dirty things, wrong things." All this belongs to the Anti-Christ, because it is the time of the Anti-Christ and those devils are preparing people to be owned by them.[25]

Shaykh Nazim has attributed his presence in England specifically to the blessing of its Royal Family, and concerning HRH Prince Charles, he has said: "He is on the right path, even though devils are trying to stop him...He is brave, because he is from the line of the Prophet. He is a Defender of Truth."[26]

The Golden Chain of the Naqshbandi Order is now known also as Haqqani, after Shaykh Nazim al-Haqqani, and "Defender of Truth" approximates the significance of this title. "Nazim" means "arranger." "I am looking for people who are true enough to defend truth," Shaykh Nazim explained in an interview, "That is my target: to find Truth Defenders and make them into a big mass. To attack the satanic kingdom

---

[24] The "Last Testament" is the Holy Qur'an.

[25] *When Will Peace Come to Earth?*, 1991, pages 28-30.

[26] *Defending Truth*, 1997, page 83. Shaykh Nazim explained this designation previously: "Prince Charles says that he is the Defender of Faith, but a faith can be wrong or right...You must be defenders of truth. Everyone believes in so many beliefs, but they are not all true just because you think so. There is a reality, only one, only one truth. It could be that you are living in an imagination...May the satanic ways and beliefs be taken away. May the lights of real faith be established and everyone become sincere servants of the Lord Almighty" (*Secret Desires*, 1996, page 152).

and to bring it down and to establish the Heavenly Sovereignty on earth."[27] On the subject of this sovereignty, he has been more specific, saying, "a new group is evolving until the coming of Jesus Christ. He has asked them to be called the 'Legion of the Royal Kingdom of Jesus on earth.' He wants every real believer of Muslims and Christians to be servants of his Royal Kingdom, because it will be the Kingdom of Heavens on earth."[28]

Such a convergence of Muslim and Christian piety has been prefigured, with eschatological significance, in the veneration of the Companions of the Cave. Concerning the nine points of spiritual inspiration, the last point is described as a return to the cave as mentioned in the story of the Companions of the Cave in the Holy Qur'an, and so the saint representing this microcosmic point partakes of the quality of these Companions. As mentioned above, the Companions of the Cave are above all exemplars of spiritual chivalry. The Seal of Spiritual Chivalry al-Mahdi, along with his seven wazirs, all possess nine spiritual qualities that are described by Shaykh Muhyiuddin Ibn al-`Arabi. Since the designation "Two Wings" refers to the saints of the nine points, the White Crown of Gondor with its two wings, borne by Frodo of the Nine Fingers in the coronation of the King, may be understood as confirming the nine qualities of the Mahdi and his wazirs; they in turn are represented in the crown's ornamentation of "seven gems of adamant" and the "single jewel" of its summit.

The emergence of the Companions from the cave signifies the appearance of a long hidden sanctity, when "light from the shadows shall spring;" and so in terms of eschatology it signals the Golden Age. Remarkably, the fortieth master of the Chain of Gold has announced the location of the Mahdi and his companions: "(in Arabia) there is a huge cave. Inside that cave there is the Dome of Happiness,[29] which has been

---

[27] 1997, page 82.
[28] *Pure Hearts*, 1998, page 57. Still, while the word "legion" recalls the Roman military, he is very clear on the subject of military struggle or jihad: "There can be no jihad until Imam Mehdi comes. Those who are proclaiming the right to declare jihad now, are liars" (*Star from Heaven*, 1996, page 26). Shaykh Nazim visited Rome in 1994.
[29] Here the terms "cave" and "dome" recall the meaning of "Elrond," in whose house Aragorn was raised until the time of his appearance.

built by angels. Mahdi `alayhi Salam[30] and his 99 Caliphs are there. They are waiting and expecting the Holy Command of Allah Almighty to appear."[31]

---

[30] This phrase means "peace be upon him," and should follow any mention of holy personages in keeping with proper manners in Islam.

[31] *The Secrets Behind the Secrets Behind the Secrets...*, 1986, page 143. Another remarkable statement may be not unrelated to the eschatological significance of the Court of the Lions in the Alhambra: "When Mahdi (peace be upon him) comes, twelve thousand soldiers from five countries in the west (known only to the awliya') will come. Those twelve thousand are always in contact with Divine powers, a sign of real faith. They are forever steadfast, never turning their faces from the face of Allah Almighty under any circumstances. Armies turn to ashes under their gaze. They are descendants of Sayyidina `Ali..." (*Mercy Oceans*, 1980, page 39).

12

Some Conclusions

During the course of writing *The Lord of the Rings*, J.R.R. Tolkien came to know the author Charles Williams in the small literary circle at Oxford known as the Inklings. Williams had formerly been a member of A.E. Waite's Fellowship of the Rosy Cross; yet despite the Catholic leanings of Waite, Williams left the order to devote himself more fully to the Anglican Church. Still, his writings betray a profound concern with Hermeticism, and in the novel *Many Dimensions*, Williams presents Hermeticism in the context of mystical Islam. That is not all, for this novel concerns a struggle to possess a Solomonic talisman, the "Stone of the King;" indeed it must be admitted that very many of the story's details resonate remarkably with the particular themes addressed in these pages.[1] Yet Tolkien denied any influence between he and Williams, and while there is no reason to doubt this, since the Hermetic traditions of Islam exist independently from these two men, it becomes rather inconceivable that Professor Tolkien could be ignorant of these traditions, when confronted by Williams' knowledge of them. And given Williams' background in Hermeticism, it must also be observed that he was for some reason the second of only two Inklings – the other being

---

[1] To provide some examples, this Stone – the first created substance - is associated not only with Solomon – called a commander of the Faithful – but with Adam in Paradise, the crown of Lucifer, and the Sakinah; with Imperial Rome, seven caliphs, and the legacy of Islam in Spain. It is far-seeing and healing, which the faithful are enjoined to guard and not to use, and the destruction of the Stone in a volcano is even considered. An essential theme of the story is belief, recognized by letters on the forehead. Despite these remarkable similarities, it might be argued that whereas sanctity and corruption are clearly distinguished in Tolkien's work, Williams offers no such clarity in his treatment of the Stone and its heritage.

C.S. Lewis – to whom Tolkien consistently presented his work in progress for approval.

Of course, because of its heritage, Alchemy naturally transcends the distinctions of Aryan and Semitic; and despite the charge of racism against *The Lord of the Rings*, it must be recognized that Tolkien's work united the noblest aspirations of the "Aryan peoples" with Abrahamic religiosity at a time when the campaign of Aryan Fascism against Semitism became so terrible. The evolution of Tolkien's alchemy should at the same time not be isolated from a remarkable contemporary development in European thought, heralded by the writings of René Guénon. In the late 1920s, Guénon was a contributor to a publication called *Regnabit* that shared with Tolkien a perspective both Catholic and monarchist. Appearing in *Regnabit* was an essay by Guénon on the legend of the Holy Grail, in which the Grail is identified with the emerald of Lucifer's fall as well as with the symbolism of the book, that concludes with an affirmation of the Primordial Tradition, "the consciousness of which has at times been obscured among men but which has never entirely disappeared."[2] Another publication belonging to the same period and sharing contributors with *Regnabit* was *Atlantis*; indeed, for Guénon, the ancient Atlantis was a particular development of this Primordial Tradition. Furthermore, for Guénon the downfall of Atlantis followed the revolt of the representatives of worldly power against the guidance of Heaven, and it must be recognized that this is precisely the meaning of Tolkien's account of Atalantë and the war of Ar-Pharazôn against Aman.[3] There should be no doubt that in his account of Atlantis and the remnants of its faithful, as well as in his Elfstone image of the Grail, Tolkien is likewise affirming the Primordial Tradition, not in doctrinal explanation[4] but in mythic imagination, for a

---

[2] Guénon adds that in the search for signs of this Tradition, "the points of comparison multiply as if by themselves and new proofs appear at every moment" ("The Sacred Heart and the Legend of the Holy Grail," reprinted in *Fundamental Symbols of Sacred Science*).

[3] It should be observed that the memory of Atlantis yet endures mostly because of a fascination with its superior technology, and, as Tolkien has quite rightly observed, technology – or in his words, the Machine – is "more closely related to Magic than is usually recognized" (*Letters*, number 131). Such a fascination, of course, misleads Saruman in his Númenórean tower.

[4] One aspect of doctrine which Tolkien does explain informs the "Standing Silence" of the Faithful, in which they turn to the West "'towards Númenor that

time in which that Tradition had become obscured as never before due to the disintegration of traditional life.

While Tolkien was writing *The Lord of the Rings*, Guénon published his great work called *The Reign of Quantity and the Signs of the Times*, a remarkable description of the Great Parody that opposes Tradition and signals the end of the world, a description which may be profitably compared with Tolkien's image of the Dark Lord. During this same period, Martin Lings, having taken a degree in English at Oxford University, became acquainted with Guénon at his home in Egypt. So it was that in 1994 HRH Prince Charles asked Lings, a respected continuator of Guénon's writings on Tradition,[5] to address the Prince of Wales Institute on the subject of René Guénon. Lings included this summary in his address:

> To sum up what his function was, one might say that it was his function, in a world increasingly rife with heresy and pseudo religion, to remind twentieth century man of the need for orthodoxy which itself presupposes firstly a divine intervention, and secondly a tradition which hands down with

---

was, and beyond to Elvenhome that is, and to that which is beyond Elvenhome and will ever be'" ("The Window on the West"). Tolkien's word here for "silence" in its hallowed aspect is "din," the Arabic word for religion. This ritual of the Faithful may be compared with what Guénon describes in another contribution to *Regnabit*: "We refer to ritual orientation, which is properly the direction towards a spiritual center, a terrestrial and perceptible image of the veritable 'Center of the World'...In Islam, this orientation (qiblah) is the materialization, if one may speak thus, of the intention (niyyah) by which all the powers of the being must be directed towards the Divine Principle..." ("The Idea of the Center in the Traditions of Antiquity," reprinted in *Fundamental Symbols of Sacred Science*). Incidentally, there is in the ancient history of the Holy Ka`ba the account of an infidel king's futile invasion, and the only defense of this spiritual center of Islam appeared in the form of supernatural birds. Tolkien provides a very similar account concerning Ar-Pharazôn's invasion of Aman, in which only the "Eagles of Manwë" are arrayed against the tyrant king. In both cases these tyrants employed the mightiest military power of the time, the elephant (al-fil) against the Ka`ba, the ship Alcarondas against Aman.

[5] It should not be overlooked that Lings is also the author of the best study of the significance of Shakespeare's plays, *The Sacred Art of Shakespeare* (Inner Traditions, 1998), to which was recently added a forward by HRH The Prince of Wales.

> fidelity from generation to generation what Heaven has
> revealed. In this connection we are deeply indebted to him for
> having restored to the world the word orthodoxy in the full
> rigor of its original meaning, that is, rectitude of opinion, a
> rectitude which compels the intelligent man not merely to
> reject heresy, but also to recognize the validity of all those
> faiths which conform to those criteria on which his own faith
> depends for its orthodoxy.

Tolkien asserted that "*The Lord of the Rings* is of course a fundamentally religious and Catholic work;"[6] yet "catholic" means universal,[7] and Tolkien without doubt expressed his religious work in the symbolic and therefore universal language of Alchemy, which has served many forms of religious orthodoxy. Given the role of Oxford as a center for the preservation of Hermeticism in Europe, Tolkien's work not surprisingly belongs to this heritage. It should also not be surprising that his work should accord so remarkably with the Hermetic writings of Wolfram and Paracelsus in Germany, for these are all forms of the "spirit" that Tolkien admitted trying to present "in its true light;" and it must be recognized that these forms share something more: an indebtedness to Islam. However, when the sciences of Hermes are divorced from religious orthodoxy, there should be no doubt that this provides but another example of the rebellion of worldly power against heavenly authority, and so is akin to the cause of Atlantis' downfall. The confusion between Hermeticism and the occult may in part account for Tolkien's silence concerning the alchemy of his great work.

According to Shaykh Nazim al-Haqqani: "You may belong to any religion...but you must follow Truth."[8] This unanimity of orthodoxy has its proper fulfillment at the end of the world, when according to the Great Master Muhyiuddin Ibn al-`Arabi, the Mahdi will restore the Pure

---

[6] *Letters*, number 142.

[7] "The word 'catholic,' taken thus in its original sense, frequently recurs in writings of more or less direct Rosicrucian inspiration," Guénon noted in his article on a characteristic sign of the original Rosicrucians, the "Gift of Tongues" (*Perspectives on Initiation*, page 234, note 4). Concerning Rosicrucian "catholicism," it should be observed that its allegiance to Rome was focused more on the Empire than on the Papacy, in part owing to its original inspiration from Islamic sources.

[8] *Op. cit.*, 1997, page 58.

Religion, as it is called in the Holy Qur'an. This is an "absolute monotheism," since "Pure Religion is for God only,"[9] purified from human innovation in the face of Truth. Now the claim of fundamentalism is to restore religion to its original purity; yet this is but a parody of the eschatological restoration. Fundamentalism is a human invention that separates religious people, and rejects the chain of transmission that connects to the transcendent, choosing instead the descent into confusion and destruction. On the other hand, it has been the legacy of mysticism to connect to the transcendent, and so the Sufis may be identified as "the living spirit of the Islamic tradition," as HRH the Prince of Wales has done. And according to Prince Charles, the books of the Sufis "deliver the message of 'Ihsan' or 'doing what is beautiful,' the antithesis of the message of hate and intolerance spouted by terrorists. I suggest that we could all, Christians, Muslims, Jews, Hindus, Sikhs and even Atheists, return to those texts with profit and humility."[10]

In a Tradition of the Prophet of Islam, the nature of Islamic fundamentalism (Wahhabism) that fuels terrorism is identified as an affliction and a "horn of the Devil" that rises from the East; such a description accords well with the Dark Tower of *The Lord of the Rings*. Tolkien himself alluded to the evils of fundamentalism in likening religion to a tree:

> The wise may know that it began with a seed, but it is vain to try and dig it up, for it no longer exists, and the virtue and powers that it had now reside in the Tree. Very good: but in husbandry the authorities, the keepers of the Tree, must look after it, according to such wisdom as they possess, prune it, remove cankers, rid it of parasites, and so forth. (With trepidation, knowing how little their knowledge of growth is!) But they will certainly do harm, if they are obsessed with the desire of going back to the seed or even to the first youth of the plant when it was (as they imagine) pretty and unafflicted by evils.[11]

It should not be surprising that Tolkien, in commenting on the renewal of the White Tree of Gondor, explained that it should therefore be

---

[9] *Qur'an*, XXXIX, 3.
[10] Quoted from a speech delivered on 11 December 2002.
[11] *Letters*, number 306.

presumed that "the worship of God would be renewed, and His Name be again more often heard."[12] Yet it is remarkable indeed that on the same page of *The Return of the King* that concerns this renewal, Tolkien mentions two place names of Gondor deriving from the same linguistic element "din," the Arabic word for religion: Amon Dîn and Rath Dînen, the Hill and Street of Din. And at that very moment in the story, Elrond reappears in glory, whom Tolkien honors with the title "master of wisdom,"[13] and who preserves the ancient wisdom older than Númenor - since the Elves are the "Firstborn" - or rather the Primordial Tradition even more ancient than Atlantis. The Pure Religion is at once the last and the first, since it is in accordance with the primordial oath; it is manifest in Idris and Muhammad and all the prophets; it is one – "only one truth" - no matter how many trees from the same source had to pass away before being supplanted.[14]

    At the opening of the twenty-first century, the mysterious significance of *The Lord of the Rings* appears on printed page and "silver screen,"[15] and reaches even into the plains of Central Asia, where in the land once ruled by the Khwajagan the events of the Third Age of Middle-earth are being reenacted. The timing of this pervasiveness even manifests a curious coincidence of dates, again in light of Islam, for the end of the Third Age of Middle-earth is reckoned as the year 1421 by the Hobbits, and this date is precisely the year of the Islamic calendar that corresponds to the end of the past millennium in the Christian calendar. Of course, the promise of a new millennium brings the hope that a new age may soon dawn, and it is the promise of eschatology that there must come the time when the outer world finally catches up to express the completion of the inner world. Certainly Tolkien's vision perceives that "in the end the Shadow is but a small and passing thing;"[16] for as it is

---

[12] *Ibid.*, number 156.

[13] Cf. appendix A of *The Lord of the Rings*.

[14] "Trees" in this sense are so many formulations of the vertical axis without which the greater mysteries of religion may not be known.

[15] However, it must be acknowledged that in its muddling – and in some alarming cases, inverting - of the story and its symbolism, the film trilogy succeeds rather in veiling Tolkien's alchemy instead of revealing it, and this is especially so regarding the cornerstone of Númenórean sanctity. Still, it may be observed that the star of the films is named Elijah, suggesting a residue of the "Eliatic function."

[16] "The Land of Shadow," *The Return of the King*.

promised in the Holy Qur'an, "Truth comes and falsehood vanishes; lo! falsehood is ever bound to vanish."[17] That this sanctification of the world is achieved like an alchemical process is alluded to in the Traditions of the Prophet of Islam: "At the end of time there will be a trial in which people will be sorted in a way similar to the way in which gold is sorted from metal." Indeed in this "Novel of the Century," it is in relation to the "antichristic talisman" of the One Ring, with its golden allure mocking the alchemical gold of the perfected world and soul, that its characters are sorted either as friends of faith or of a one-eyed Enemy of the Faithful. In the Holy Qur'an, the message for the faithful is clear: "O you who believe! Be aware of God and be with the truthful."[18] It may be said that it is by holding to this teaching through eschatological trials that Tolkien's "little people" are illumined by a Western Sun, which is of course the primary concern of Tolkien's "hobbito-centric" narrative: "the ennoblement (or sanctification) of the humble."[19] Inasmuch as "The Downfall of the Lord of the Rings and the Return of the King" is the "Red Book," Tolkien's story with its symbolism has become an alchemical elixir. For the mystics of Islam, "elixir" signifies the Truth that transmutes an unbeliever into a believer.

According to J.R.R. Tolkien: "Every writer making a secondary world wishes in some measure to be a real maker, or hopes that he is drawing on reality: hopes that the peculiar quality of this secondary world (if not all the details) are derived from Reality, or flowing into it."[20] In a sense, Alchemy is the science by means of which the imagination flows into Reality:

> Alchemy...enlarges the dream of the individual soul to cosmic dimensions, breaking the prison of individual existence by the love of the beauty of Nature. The dream of the individual soul becomes that of the World Soul...In the end...the alchemist realizes that it is not he but the Divine Principle of the universe that is truly dreaming the cosmos.[21]

---

[17] XVII, 81.
[18] IX, 119.
[19] *Letters*, number 181.
[20] Carpenter, *op. cit.*, page 195.
[21] Nasr, *Science and Civilization in Islam*, Plume, 1970, page 246.

Springing from England, a kingdom neither Catholic nor belonging to the lands of Islam yet under the patronage of St. George,[22] his story has been welcomed by a world in need of healing. On the author's tombstone in Oxfordshire, the name "Beren" is engraved with his own. In Tolkien's fantasy, it was Beren who, hidden by a monstrous appearance, wrested the silmaril from the crown of Morgoth. Like Beren, Tolkien has reclaimed a primordial treasure – a universal language - even while maintaining the appearance of fantasy. In so doing the Thrice-great identity of Hermes is restored; so too is the reality of the Grail, raised like a cornerstone in Aragorn's final appearance: "Then Aragorn took the green stone and held it up, and there came a green fire from his hand."[23] This primordial treasure is not other than that vouchsafed to the Haqqani Order, and defended by the Prince of Wales. From a first evocation of John the Baptist in a star, to the unveiling of a "Kingdom of Heaven on Earth" by an Elias foretold, a light of sanctity shines through Tolkien's writings.

> When the terrestrial globe – to pick up once more the thread of our symbolism – begins to crack, according to the traditional teachings, fissures occur not only "below," but also "above." Through the upper fissures, which represent openings of Good and of Grace in the face of the evil arising from the abysses, there penetrates a spiritual light which can enlighten the "hearts of the children" of Adam and bring them back to the "hearts of the fathers," to the spirituality of the traditions...The true "Eliatic current" will intensify, according to Scripture, in direct proportion to the progressive darkening of the world, and it will continue to do so to the very last moment.[24]

---

[22] In Ottoman lands, St. George (al-Khidr) and Elias were so closely associated that their names were conjoined in the name of the spring festival Hidrellez.

[23] "Many Partings."

[24] Schaya, op. cit., pages 39-40. Concerning such fissures, the worldwide phenomenon known as Crop Circles may be offered as physical proof, and this phenomenon has been centered very precisely in England since the passing of Professor Tolkien. Now the Hermetic significance of a landscape mysteriously becoming "spiritualized" by these circular symbols has not escaped some researchers. That many circles are hoaxes, or rather parodies, itself suggests the importance of the real phenomenon.

And so more than being a mere work of imagination, *The Lord of the Rings* is an unrivalled work of inspiration, and may play a not insignificant role in preparing people worldwide for events that do not belong to some legendary Middle-earth; in the light of faith, these events of this Earth only come nearer with every passing moment.

Index

www.ingramcontent.com/pod-product-compliance
Lightning Source LLC
Chambersburg PA
CBHW030524100426
42813CB00001B/147